when
DIVORCE
happens

A Guide for Family and Friends

when DIVORCE happens

James Greteman, C.S.C.
and Joseph Dunne, Ph.D.

AVE MARIA PRESS   Notre Dame, Indiana 46556

James Greteman, C.S.C., is a clinical marriage and family therapist with the Catholic Charities office in Salina, Kansas, a position he also held with the diocese of Sioux City, Iowa. He is a member of the American Association of Marriage and Family Therapists and holds a Master's Degree from the University of Notre Dame. He has authored numerous articles and booklets and is co-author of *Divorce and Beyond* (ACTA Publications, 1984).

Joseph Dunne is a professional writer and editor residing in Skokie, Illinois. He earned a Master's Degree from De Paul University and a Ph.D. from the University of Notre Dame.

Excerpts from THE NEW JERUSALEM BIBLE, copyright © 1985 by Darton, Longman & Todd, Ltd. and Doubleday & Company, Inc. Reprinted by permission of the publisher.

© 1990 by Ave Maria Press, Notre Dame, IN 46556

International Standard Book Number: 0-87793-427-4

Library of Congress Catalog Card Number: 90-81942

Cover and text design by Katherine Robinson Coleman.

Printed and bound in the United States of America.

Contents

Dedication

—To my co-author, Joe Dunne, for making some sense out of my ideas;
—To my family in Iowa for always giving love;
—To my religious community for caring and compassion;
—To my friends for direction;
—To my divorced friends who taught me about holiness (wholeness)

—*James Greteman*

To Jim Greteman, for practicing the ''availability,'' patience and encouragement that he preaches; my parents, Joseph, Sr., and Margaret, for their sacrifices and example; the Vincentian Fathers for invaluable training; National Marriage Encounter and my Dialogue Group, for insights into marriage and human relations; Mike and Linda Voitik for a story; and Patricia, Susan and Carolyn, a major part of my ''tapestry.'' Their influence contributed to this book but even more to my life.

—*Joseph Dunne*

Introduction

"My family and friends love me, but they don't understand why I've divorced."

"I often fly off the handle or withdraw into myself, and I can see that this hurts my family and friends. I wish I could help them understand what I'm going through and how much I love them and need them."

Divorced people frequently say such things as they sort through their pain and attempt to reorder their lives. Having lost the person closest to them, they need the love of parents, children, brothers, sisters, relatives and friends more than ever. These people can provide stability and also help fill the sudden void in the life of a divorced person.

This book seeks to help these relatives and friends understand the turmoil a divorcing person experiences. It also suggests ways of helping them rebuild their lives. Those who divorce typically go through intense emotional reactions for more than a year. It may take up to five years to establish a new identity completely. Major changes may include a new job, a new dwelling, new neighborhood, new friends and neighbors, and a new church. They need support in this time of struggle and change.

We know how painful it is to see people hurting, especially the people we love. Usually, our first impulse is to want to take away the trouble and the pain. Americans are big on fixing things. Countless books, television shows and classes are devoted to fixing homes, cars and appliances. Unfortunately, we cannot "fix" people. So often our most well-intentioned efforts seem to backfire by stirring the hurting person's anger or leading to withdrawal.

Many people regard free advice as being worth every penny they pay for it. Typically, telling people what to do is a waste of time. Nevertheless, on some occasions, a person may need a little push, either away from a self-destructive course or into a needed action. We suggest ways you might convey suggestions indirectly, allowing others to draw their own conclusions without feeling "bossed."

There are no magic words or other quick fixes. But concerned family and friends can certainly help the divorced. Perhaps the most important way is simply to show that you accept them, even if you do not approve of divorce in general or of their actions. Understanding what they are going through will help you to be accepting. This book begins with a description of the causes and typical progression of many divorces.

Next, we will look at some typical concerns many have about divorce. Does befriending a person going through a divorce indicate that you approve of divorce? Are you thereby encouraging the breakup of the basic unit of society and the weakening of religious values? Will you be forced to "take sides," even though you love both the husband and the wife going through the divorce?

The pain of divorce is like a wound that the person is afraid to touch. It may need direct attention, in addition to time and self-healing. Too vigorous an attempt to help, however, may tear the wound further. Even when you begin to understand what your divorcing friend is going through and genuinely want to help, what can you do when he or she goes into seclusion or into an unresponsive depression? We offer some ways of "being there," of gently leading the divorced into non-threatening groups and activities that help them broaden their interests, discover new friends and get on with establishing a new life.

Instead of withdrawal, your friend may seethe with anger, deliver long tirades against the ex-spouse and project this anger in all directions, including yours. Excessive blaming and churning leads to immobility. You face the challenge of helping your friend channel the energy of this anger into the positive efforts needed for rebuilding.

Thus far we have focused directly on the divorcing couple and on the issue of divorce itself. But the situation in which you find yourself extends beyond this. Acute problems are faced by the children whose parents are divorcing, especially younger children. As a grandparent, aunt or uncle or close friend of the family, you may find the children turning to you in their bewilderment. We explain some of their major concerns—for example, feeling responsible for the divorce or the fear of being abandoned. Then we suggest ways of talking to them about the divorce and their concerns.

Divorce is typically part of a larger problem in psychological and emotional health. The problems that flared up in the marriage may be intense instances of more general problems that affect a person's relationships with other relatives and friends. Two important considerations flow from this. First, the divorcing person needs to overcome these problems in order to find wholeness and happiness in the future. Second, as a relative or friend, you may be entwined in the problem.

To take a simplified example, someone who had difficulty expressing love toward parents and siblings may find it difficult to express love toward a spouse. By working on your own relationship with the person, you may be able to help him or her overcome a problem that could continue to undermine their attempts to establish stable relationships.

This last step goes far beyond external words of encouragement or "little acts of kindness," important though these be. It certainly means deepening your relationship with the divorcing person. It will likely mean exploring the unfinished business in your own life, as well as in the life of the other person. In the process, you will both grow.

This book has emerged from the concerns of the many people who have sought counselling during the past 15 years. It is filled with stories of real people and offers practical help in dealing with the issues and concerns of divorce. Working with divorced people in individual counselling sessions, small discussion groups and large seminars has brought insight into their difficulties and helped fashion methods that work. This book seeks to provide this information in a developed and readily available form.

Like all of life's sorrows and difficulties, divorce is something no one would wish upon themselves or others. When dealt with positively, however, it can offer opportunities to mature and enlarge one's horizons. Both the people going through a divorce and those who care about them and support them will find that good can emerge from a painful experience.

The task is not easy, but neither is it beyond any determined person's means. You can take courage from the knowledge that the rewards, both for the one you care about and for yourself, are great. Gentleness and patience, both with the divorcing and with yourself, are the keys.

1

The Story

The church was brightly decorated with coordinated flower arrangements and banks of glowing candles, all dedicated to this special event. People smiled and gestured welcomes as they settled into the pews. Long-separated friends and relatives eagerly embraced and exchanged news. Here and there, amateur photographers intently adjusted their cameras to preserve this festive moment forever. Heads turned repeatedly toward the back of the church for a glimpse of the bride.

Besides the pleasure of renewing old ties, beyond the pageantry of the decorations and the elegant clothes of the participants and their guests, those present felt a sense of family and ongoing tradition—the older people with their memories of several generations; the middle-aged ones with their families and careers in full swing; and the younger ones with their plans for the future.

At last the organ resounded with the wedding march. The flower girl in her formal gown, carrying a child's straw basket, led the procession. With cadenced step, the bridesmaids and maid of honor, wearing full-sized versions of the flower girl's gown, followed at measured intervals. Finally the bride swept into the aisle, a vision of white in lace veil and trailing gown. Necks strained and flashbulbs flared to capture her shining eyes and shy smile. The straining and flashing intensified as the bride and groom joined at the altar.

The ceremony flowed beautifully. Even the flower girl and the ring bearer tripping over the same step seemed to add just the right personal touch. As they witnessed the exchange of vows, relatives and friends of the couple felt their world reaffirmed and enlarged. A person close to them was now "settled," would have love and support and could look forward to enjoying a family. The new spouse would enlarge the circle of family and friends—the son or daughter the parents had never had or a "fourth" for "couple activities." Two whole families would now be linked, further enlarging the circle.

The wedding also gave a renewed sense of security to other couples among the guests. The new couple was reaffirming the importance and value of marriage. The large number of people attending and the prominence the church gave to the ceremony further attested to its value.

After the ceremony, the reception, the meal and the dancing, the family and friends of the new couple left for their homes with a warm feeling of reassurance and stability.

Several years later, the couple has a child who is beginning to bring comprehensible stories and recognizable pictures home from school and a toddler with a charming smile whose eagerness to master talking regularly results in entertaining mistakes in the use and pronunciation of common words.

The couple and their children have become an integral part of major occasions in both families—holidays, weddings and funerals—and regular callers and hosts at other times for parents, brothers and sisters, special aunts and uncles and close cousins. Each partner now has a new identity as a fully matured person, a co-head of society's basic social unit, a part of a "team."

Some relatives and friends live in other parts of the country and their face-to-face meetings with the couple are rare, but the couple still writes an annual Christmas letter and sends a family photograph with it.

The important milestones that follow the wedding are captured and neatly displayed in the photo albums of the couple and their friends and relatives. Like story-books, these albums of smiling people and joyful memories leave those who turn their pages with a ''happily-ever-after'' feeling.

smoke bomb to Tom Soedye potato
to Judge Mac comments to
excessive drinking to refusal to
share # to

2

The Myth: "And They Lived Happily Ever After"

Everyone knows that even the best marriages have difficult times—partners become impatient with each other, feel the stress of too much to do and no time for themselves or become embroiled in a struggle with their children. A young couple may be in love and have a beautiful personal relationship, but that alone does not solve all of life's difficulties. Their failure to solve these problems may eventually signal the end of the marriage.

In some cases, the break comes abruptly. Greg, a trucker and the father of nine children, called from out of state to inform his wife, Betty, that he had filed for a divorce. In other cases, a couple is unable to cope with a major crisis or a series of crises.

Much more commonly—in about 90 percent of the cases—the partners gradually build up walls between themselves. Hidden resentments, "touchy" subjects they don't want to discuss, interests they don't care to share are all like individual bricks: It is easy to step over or around one or two, but as the bricks mount they form a wall that imprisons each person and closes out the other. Ironically, each person is usually more conscious of the other's wall, and resentment over that leads to further work on his or her own wall.

Jack and Bev, a couple in their middle 40s, provide a typical example. Both had been struggling with mid-life crises when Jack's business began having financial problems. One trait they had in common was a disinclination to tell others about their problems or to seek professional help. They also took their relationship for granted. As their stress grew, they turned their energies to other concerns: Jack to his business; Bev to their three children. In the end, their relationship seemed to have died.

By the time they realized what had happened, they lacked any tools to put their relationship back together. They began to fight verbally just to get some private space. The fights and the distancing in turn increased their resentment toward each other, until all they had left was a negative relationship. One day, Jack announced that he could not take it any more and moved out. Bev felt deeply hurt and worried what would become of her after 24 years of marriage.

However the divorce comes about, and whether or not it was anticipated, it usually comes as a shock to the spouses, their friends and their relatives. Though people generally acknowledge that divorce has become increasingly common, many somehow feel that it is a phenomenon that affects only others. Surprise can leave one unprepared to deal with divorce.

Moreover, divorce is a wrenching experience. It is, to begin with, based upon rejection, for at least one of the spouses has expressed a desire to leave the other. Very commonly, the decision to leave is itself based upon a feeling of having been emotionally rejected—an awareness of the other's "bricks."

Divorce also disrupts most social relationships. Typically, each spouse will be cut off from the other's lifelong friends and relatives. Each may often find, even among his or her own relatives and lifelong friends, a sense of strangeness. The divorced person no longer forms part of a team, the archetypal social unit, and cannot simply resume a ''young single'' role.

Both will probably also find themselves no longer invited to the homes of some couples with whom they had regularly made up foursomes. An unattached person may be regarded as a potential threat to the other relationship or, more simply, inviting only one person may mean that there is no fourth for bridge or that one of the other couple has no one to talk with.

The divorced couple face many other difficulties as well. At least one of them will have to find a new place to live. Typically, one will have to cope with the children alone, while the other will be largely cut off from them. In most cases, each will have less money to live on, since their income will be divided and will have to keep two households going. And each will have to learn to do the jobs that the other usually took care of.

Add to these factors the feelings of failure, of guilt, of a loss of an important part of one's identity, of reduced social acceptability (real or imagined), and the result is an insecure, confused person who finds it difficult to interact easily with others. By turns, the divorced person may manifest many moods—withdrawn, angry, guilt-ridden, tearful, blaming.

The divorced person can be difficult to deal with. Relatives and friends can easily feel that they are being unfairly snubbed or ''dumped upon,'' or become ''gun-shy''—worried that a simple poor choice of a word will cause a sudden shift in mood.

It is also typical for family members and friends to struggle with strong emotions of their own. In many respects, divorce is like a wedding in reverse: Whereas the wedding was a sharing of the couple's joy, an enlarging of the circle and an affirmation of family values and social stability, the divorce is a sharing of the couple's sorrow, a narrowing of the circle and an apparent abandonment of commitment to family stability.

As a family member or friend, then, you will play an important part in the divorcing person's struggles to adjust to a new state in life. Rejection or simple avoidance on your part will further destabilize that person's world, while continued love and caring interaction can offer a point of stability and continuity.

Offering this continued caring can prove difficult. You may find yourself struggling with both the volatile emotions of the divorcing person and your own, perhaps subconscious, feelings. You are likely to experience feelings of personal loss, of insecurity—things seem a little less stable and the possibility of a divorce may now seem a little closer to home.

You may also feel that the divorce is foolish or blameworthy. Some people may see one or both divorcing persons as being at fault—their alcoholism, or gambling, or love affairs caused the breakup. Others may have a more general concern that people are divorcing too easily—flouting God's law, hurting their families and destabilizing society. Such feelings may create a fear that in seeking to comfort a divorced person one thereby condones divorce.

On the other hand, others may feel more like congratulating one of the ex-spouses on finally getting rid of a bad partner. This may conflict with the divorced person's mixed feelings over the end of a significant part of his or her life.

Still others may offer strong feelings of pity that fail to move the divorced person into more constructive ways of dealing with the reality and getting on with life.

We will examine these attitudes in detail further on. For the present, consider the example of Jesus: He spoke kindly to the woman at the well, who had had five husbands and was living with yet another man (Jn 4:7-30). The important thing is to speak kindly to the divorced couple, their families, relatives and friends. There can be healing for all as they continue their journey to God. Go gently.

3

The Tapestry
of Our Lives

To understand what happens in a divorce, we have to appreciate the extent to which our lives are interwoven with each other's. Even people we have never met have changed our lives—civil wars in countries halfway around the world from us have influenced our elections, changed our economy and forced us to re-examine our values; a handful of people who poisoned a few packages of food and medicine have affected millions of people who work for the manufacturers, own their stock or find a favorite product either no longer available or higher-priced.

On a more personal level, few would question that families, friends, neighbors, fellow parishioners and business associates strongly influence each other. But the circle of influence extends far beyond our intimates. Someone once said, we should choose our enemies carefully, for we are likely to become like them.

Jesus frequently stressed that our lives are inseparable from those of our neighbors—that we are all branches on the true vine, sharing God's life (Jn 15:1-8); that love of God and neighbor constitute the great commandments (Mk 12:28-34); that indeed our final judgment hinges upon our helping, or failing to help, our neighbor (Mt 25:31-46).

Whether we look at personal interactions from an economic, political, social, psychological or religious point of view, we find, as John Donne wrote in the 17th century:

> No man is an island, entire of itself; every man is a piece of the continent, a part of the main; if a clod be washed away by the sea, Europe is the less, as well as if a promontory were, as well as if a manor of thy friend's or of thine own were ("Meditation XVII," *Devotions Upon Emergent Occasions*).

People often appear to lack individual identities. Ask "who" people are, and the answer is likely to be a series of relationships—the companies they work for, the persons they are married to, the parents they are the children of, the children they are the parents of, the persons they are the friends of, the neighborhoods they live in and so forth. A somewhat more individual trait might be added as an afterthought—they are bright, friendly, witty, artistic, persevering, political, spiritual. Rarely, however, are such traits elaborated upon and strung together to form the principal description.

Such traits often seem like so many loose threads: A few might catch the casual eye now and then, but, as a whole, it is only when they are woven into a tapestry that their beauty is fully appreciated. Our lives appear to others as a series of pictures, like those on a large tapestry covering a castle wall, providing both protection from drafts and an artistry that puts meaning and beauty into a drab environment. Just as a tapestry is made of conjoined threads, so our public lives are made up of our interactions with others—the interweaving of our threads with those of others. For most people, one of the largest and most important scenes is their married life.

When the couple divorce, they pull many of their threads from a major scene in each other's tapestry.

Other withdrawals almost always follow. When Jack and Bev separated, the children stayed with Bev; Jack only saw them on visits. The two younger children, Terri, 16, and John, 13, had the most difficult time dealing with this separation, because their parents' home still formed their base. Terri in particular felt that her parents had betrayed the values that they had tried to instill in her, so she became aloof from both of them.

Relatives from both sides of the family did not know what to say to their former brother- or sister-in-law when they happened to meet. Some would say, "I miss you," while others would pass by without saying anything.

With a divorce, many of the threads interwoven by others are abruptly pulled from one's tapestry, leaving many important scenes looking damaged or threadbare. Other people may react to this in many ways—outrage, sorrow, shame, pity, probably all based upon the interpretation that the tapestry is ruined.

This perception can lead to further damage to other pictures and even to the very backing of the tapestry, one's self-love and self-esteem. Betty had regularly attended the seven o'clock Mass on Sunday morning, where she and her nine children had always taken up the gifts. Some weeks after Greg, her trucker husband, had divorced her, several ushers came up to her and asked her not to take up the gifts any more. It was as though she had become bad, or that her church had divorced her as well.

Similarly, a man who served on various deacon boards found that the divorced were the subject of frequent, prolonged discussions:

> Angry board members denounced all the divorced, raising difficult questions at each meeting. Could "they" serve in an official capacity? . . . Could "they" become church members? Sing in the choir? Iron bars steeled these "second-class Christians" from full fellowship

and service (Margaret Johnson, *Divorce Is a Family Affair*, p. 51).

As more pictures are rended by the withdrawal of others' threads, the tapestry appears increasingly shabby. In viewing their own situation, both what they can see themselves and what they see reflected in others' eyes, divorcing people may conclude that the work of a lifetime is gone, and that they have to rip out all of their threads and start weaving a totally new tapestry—new family, friends, neighbors, job, skills.

Most of us find tackling one new area (moving to a new neighborhood, starting a new job, getting married, taking care of a new child) to be stressful enough when the rest of our life is secure, so that we still feel competent in most matters and can enjoy times of relaxation. Without some secure places, some feeling of enduring accomplishment and self-worth, the adjustments can seem overwhelming. Restoring our tapestry may seem impossible, or not worth the effort.

One of the first ways to help divorcing people is to deal with their sense of ruination. Start with your own perception, for you are unlikely to be convincing that "things aren't so bad as they look" if you, in fact, believe that things really are that bad or even worse.

Start by considering the threadbare scenes. True, some pictures may be beyond repair, and others may be greatly altered in the restoration process. It is a mistake, however, to confuse the integrity of the threads with that of the scenes they weave. The withdrawal of others' threads does not render the remaining threads useless. In less figurative language, all of the character traits, skills, knowledge, and experiences that divorcing people once had woven into their marriages still remain a part of them and can be used again.

This is not to say that the tapestry can be restored to its earlier state, or even that all of its beauties will be realized in slightly altered form. New scenes will call for different threads—everyone acts differently within different relationships (boss, subordinate, parent, child, friend, neighbor) and with different kinds of people (some people one can laugh and be silly with, others may elicit more philosophical discussions; some call for casual conversations, others for sharing one's deepest feelings).

In weaving new relationships, then, some of the threads left from a "ruined" relationship may be reused, others may have to be put away, and still others, heretofore left unused, may play an important part in weaving new scenes. In doing so, people discover new dimensions of themselves. They also discover new dimensions of other people who begin to weave new scenes with them.

Thus far, we have considered only the changes in the divorcing person's tapestry. Our own scenes will change as well. In some cases, this will present an opportunity for our own growth. As we shall see in the chapter on "unfinished business," our own relationship—our own scenes with a divorcing person—may have been flawed, perhaps even in ways that affected or at least paralleled the marital difficulties. A mutual repair of a shared scene might offer a chance for mutual help. Helping a divorcing person is often not merely an other-directed operation, one where we act as a doctor administering to another's illness.

Divorce, like other disasters, is not something to be sought out. Once we face a disaster, however, it challenges us to grow far beyond what anyone else or we ourselves had imagined possible. As William James put it:

Most people live, whether physically, intellectually or morally, in a very restricted circle of their potential being. They *make use* of a very small portion of their possible consciousness, and of their soul's resources in general, much like a man who, out of his whole bodily organism, should get into a habit of using and moving only his little finger. Great emergencies and crises show us how much greater our vital resources are than we had supposed (Letter to W. Lutaslawski, May 6, 1906).

A first step, then, in developing a more helpful attitude toward a divorcing person is to see not a ruined tapestry but one with great potential for weaving new, richer scenes. By encouraging the person to begin work anew, and by offering some of our own threads, we can greatly help the process. We may even find opportunities for self-enrichment. As Carl Rogers put it:

The degree to which I can create relationships which facilitate the growth of others as separate persons is a measure of the growth I have achieved in myself. In some respects this is a disturbing thought, but it is also a promising or challenging one. It would indicate that if I am interested in creating helping relationships I have a fascinating lifetime job ahead of me, stretching and developing my potentialities in the direction of growth (*On Becoming a Person*, p. 56).

4

Encouragement

Discouragement over a divorce and its aftermath can lead to far worse damage. The divorcing person may decide that no one is to be completely trusted, even God; or that life is threatening; or that all joys are illusory. Instead of having one or a few tapestry scenes damaged, all of the threads of a given color, or of several colors, may be pulled out of every scene.

Worse yet, the very foundation of the tapestry, self-love, may be seriously weakened or even torn. Without this foundation, new scenes would be woven in air, and the threads of already existing scenes would sag into formless, lifeless blurs. The psychological implications are spelled out by Abraham Maslow:

> Satisfaction of the self-esteem need leads to feelings of self-confidence, worth, strength, capability, and adequacy, of being useful and necessary in the world. But thwarting of these needs produces feelings of inferiority, of weakness, and of helplessness. These feelings in turn give rise to either basic discouragement or else compensatory or neurotic trends (A.H. Maslow, *Motivation and Personality*, p. 91).

Very often, divorced persons who become uncharacteristically unpleasant (moody, withdrawn, argumentative, bitter) act defensively because they have lost their self-esteem and self-confidence. Helping them to regain their self-esteem is the necessary first repair. Once they have a strong backing, they can reweave the threads of their better selves and begin weaving new scenes involving others.

A few quick words of reassurance and a slap on the back reverberate hollowly in even a mildly discouraged person. To *feel* worthwhile, I need both external and internal approval. External approval comes from experiencing love from others; internal approval comes from a sense of competence, from experiencing success in matters that I deem to be important.

Love is expressed in many different ways, but one essential quality is that it be sustained over time. If all another person offers is a few words followed by a hasty departure, I will not feel that I am very important or worthwhile in that person's eyes. On the other hand, if that person continues to show deep interest over many months, even when I seem to offer little in return, I will eventually have to admit that, at least in that person's eyes, I seem of value.

Sometimes quiet, unobtrusive and sustained concern is all that a divorced person needs. This was the case with George, who joined a divorce group that met for an hour and a half every other week. The group discussed the general process of divorce, described their experiences and feelings to each other, and offered mutual encouragement. George followed the discussions with his eyes, and it was apparent that he shared many of the feelings aired by the others. Meeting after meeting, however, he sat through these exchanges without saying a word.

The group allowed George his space and never criticized him or tried to force his participation. At the end of each meeting, the good-byes and ''see you in two weeks'' exchanges included George, and, come the next meeting, he would resume his customary place. Finally, after eight months, he shared his experiences. The group did not make a big thing out of this, but merely offered him the same encouragement that they had been offering to each other all along.

With this sustained acceptance and encouragement, George was free to follow his own timetable in coming to grips with his divorce. Sometimes genuine interest and quiet encouragement are all that people need to find the courage to work out their own problems. Abraham Maslow tells of a student who sought advice about a personal problem:

> At the end of one hour, during which she talked and the therapist said *not a single word*, she had settled the problem to her own satisfaction, thanked him gratefully for his advice, and left (*Motivation and Personality*, pp. 310-311).

People also need to experience success in order to be convinced of their self-worth, their competence. Severely discouraged people may need continual encouragement and sustained interest from others before undertaking tasks that many people regularly perform with little thought, effort or sense of significant accomplishment. Sustained external support through these periods of discouragement can encourage a person to begin striving toward goals; this striving, in turn, is the necessary means of succeeding and gaining internal approval.

Diane's unkempt appearance immediately communicated her poor self-image. She had become pregnant at 17, dropped out of high school during her junior year and married Dan. Since Dan made good money as a construction worker, Diane stayed at home, raising four daughters, now married themselves, and a son, now 16.

When Diane came for counselling, Dan was divorcing her. Dan had agreed to give her custody of their son and the use of their house until the son turned 18; after that, the house was to be sold and the money divided between them.

Diane was now in her 40s, had never worked outside of the home and had never developed marketable skills. The thought of having to search for a job under these handicaps terrified her and she responded by staying in bed most of the time, worrying about her situation but doing nothing about it.

The process of growth began with listening and offering simple encouragement. One measure she agreed to take was keeping a chart on the refrigerator of all the things that she did well—even little things like boiling water for tea without burning the water.

Ever so slowly, Diane began to see value in the things that she did. After 14 months, her self-esteem had risen to the point where she began fixing herself up. With still more encouragement, she began making some plans.

The first goal was to get a high-school equivalency diploma (GED). Diane needed a lot of encouragement to sign up for the classes, and continual encouragement during each appointment to persevere. Pointing to her past achievements assured her that she had talent—she was good at raising kids, cooking, budgeting. Finally, she finished the classes and passed the equivalency test.

The combination of continuing encouragement and her own sense of accomplishment enabled Diane to begin planning a career. She decided that she wanted to be a records person on a hospital floor, and, with further encouragement, signed up for an eight-month program. With the passing of each test and course, Diane was weaving a significant new scene of achievement and was readying new threads of skills for future scenes of career and personal achievements. Diane still needed encouragement, but she finished the program with a high B average.

With yet further encouragement, she worked up her courage for going on job interviews. Here she had a setback: Neither of the two hospitals in town had an opening. She needed more encouragement to make and carry out an alternate plan: looking into doctors' offices and clinics. She finally found a job at the front desk of an office complex with six doctors. Seven months later, she had progressed through being in charge of all of the records to running the entire office.

Effective encouragement is often a simple matter of listening empathically and of helping people appreciate their own talents and accomplishments. It does not require special talents or extensive training, but it does take time—it took George eight months to share his experiences and feelings with the group, and it took Diane well over a year to make her first hesitant steps toward a career and over two and a half years in all to get a job.

Earlier, we noted how the rending of one scene was typically followed by the rending of many others. Here we see how the process can be reversed: Because self-esteem forms the backing of the tapestry, encouragement in any area has the effect of strengthening the entire tapestry, of providing the foundation for new weaving. As the threads of new skills and friendships are formed in any area, the tendency is to keep weaving the thread into other areas as well—success in one's career, for instance, can make one more relaxed and self-confident; this new attitude can help one make new friends more easily; new friends normally lead one into new social activities; the friends and social successes encourage an even more positive attitude and can lead to new career opportunities.

5

Encouraging the "Sinner"

To many, encouragement comes naturally. Their friend or relative is in trouble, and they respond with warm support. Others, however, may worry that encouragement of the divorcing person amounts to encouragement of divorce, or they may feel that the person is at fault and needs a kick in the butt more than a pat on the back.

As we shall see, sometimes divorcing persons may need some constructive criticism. However, they need psychic energy to respond to such a challenge. Your encouragement can help a divorced person build up this energy. This is especially important in the earlier stages of the divorce. Once the person has the energy and you have established yourself as someone who cares, a more challenging approach should have much better chances of succeeding—if, indeed, it is still needed.

Ben had been very close to his niece Heather all of her life. As an adolescent, Heather had been eager to grow up, marry and have a family. She began college, but soon dropped out, married Paul and, within a few years, was the mother of three children. Paul proved to be a devoted father as well as a good provider, and Ben became close to him as well. Although Heather had been eager to have children, she did not seem to take a deep

interest in them. Typically at family gatherings Paul kept
track of them and steered them away from trouble, while
Heather made the rounds visiting, apparently oblivious
of the children.

Recently, at a family wedding, Ben was shocked to
see Heather openly flirting with a musician at the wedding banquet. Paul was obviously hurt by this, and matters got so out of hand that he eventually left with the
children. Heather continued her flirtation and did not re-
join Paul until the next morning. Ben felt that Heather's
actions were reprehensible, but what he found the most
wrenching was the pain inflicted on Paul.

About six months later, Ben heard that Heather and
Paul were getting a divorce. Heather had not said anything about this or even about having troubles. One day
she casually started talking about an affair she was having and, with some bravado, added that Paul was asking
for a divorce and could have it for all she cared.

Since the divorce, Paul and Heather have alternated
days for taking care of their children—something Ben
views as being very destabilizing for the latter. Although
relatives typically remain close to the divorcing family
member and lose contact with the former in-law, Ben
found himself remaining close to Paul and treating
Heather with reserve.

In part, Ben sees her actions as blatant violations of
central ethical and moral values, and is ashamed and dis-
appointed that someone so close to him has acted in this
way. In greater part, however, he cannot help thinking
about the immense pain that Paul and the children are
experiencing. Maybe Ben could be more sympathetic toward Heather if she had been forced into marriage or had
drifted into it for want of desirable alternatives. As it is,
he keeps remembering how she had continually rejected
chances for an education and a career and had pushed to

establish the family she was now deserting. He hopes in time to be able to be more accepting of her, but his feelings are too strong for this at present.

One way of dealing with strongly negative feelings is to pray and turn the question over to Jesus (we shall discuss this at length further on). Another is to meditate on God's gentle treatment of all of our failings. The Bible gives many instances of God offering encouragement to sinners, even to the unrepentant. This "love of the sinner" frequently bothered the more legalistic-minded.

There are numerous stories about Pharisees and others taking scandal at Jesus' free association with sinners. When he was dining at a Pharisee's home, a woman who "had a bad name in the town" came in and began to wipe his feet with her hair and to anoint them (Lk 7:36-50). This caused the Pharisee to question Jesus' standing: "If this man were a prophet, he would know who this woman is that is touching him and what a bad name she has." That is, the Pharisee believed that no upright person would associate with an obviously sinful person—indeed, the upright would more likely feel obliged to punish the guilty.

Jesus did not even wait for the woman to repent and be punished before extending love to her—quite the opposite: "I tell you that her sins, many as they are, have been forgiven her, because she has shown such great love." Only because she had first received love and forgiveness was she able to repent.

Jesus reacted similarly to the woman who had been caught in the act of adultery (Jn 8:3-11). The scribes and Pharisees challenged Jesus: "In the Law Moses has ordered us to stone women of this kind. What have you got to say?" Jesus responded, "Let the one among you who is guiltless be the first to throw a stone at her." After the crowd had melted away, Jesus asked the woman: "Has no one condemned you?" "No one, sir," she replied. "Neither do I condemn you," Jesus concluded. "Go away, and from this moment sin no more."

Even in the Old Testament, which we more often associate with God punishing sinners, we find many expressions of God's mercy. One example of this is in the Book of Jonah, especially chapter four. When Jonah warned Nineveh of the impending punishment, the people responded by doing penitence. Jonah apparently believed that the city deserved punishment, for he upbraided God.

God replied: "Why should I not be concerned about Nineveh, the great city, in which there are more than a hundred and twenty thousand people who cannot tell their right hand from their left, to say nothing of all the animals?" (Jon 4:11). God's mercy is stronger than his anger, and he points out that many evil actions are caused in part by ignorance rather than willfulness (they "cannot tell their right hand from their left").

The Book of Hosea recounts that God, angered by the Israelites' turning to idolatry, declared that they would be returned to Egypt and subjected to the Assyrian king; even worse, "The sword will rage through their towns, wiping out their children, glutting itself inside their fortresses." But even as God noted their calling upon Baal, he abruptly relented:

> "Ephraim, how could I part with you?
> Israel, how could I give you up? . . .
> My heart within me is overwhelmed,
> fever grips my inmost being.
> I will not give rein to my fierce anger,
> I will not destroy Ephraim again,
> for I am God, not man,
> the Holy One in your midst
> and I shall not come to you in anger" (Hos 11:8-9).

Closely related to the theme of love of sinners is *noblesse oblige*—urging us to be better, not because we are currently vile, but because we are essentially good and will achieve happiness by living up to our true natures. For example, back in the 16th century, St. Teresa of Avila began her classic work on the spiritual life, *The Interior Castle*, by describing the "beauty and dignity of our souls."

This is based upon a major theme in the New Testament: "But to all who did accept him he gave power to become children of God" (Jn 1:12). This encourages us to live rightly by reminding us that we share God's very life—we are good, we have the strength, therefore we should live up to our "better selves." St. Paul used this same approach in exhorting the Corinthians to avoid fornication:

> Do you not realize that your bodies are members of Christ's body? . . . anyone who attaches himself to the Lord is one spirit with him.
> . . . Do you not realize that your body is the temple of the Holy Spirit, who is in you and whom you received from God? (1 Cor 6:15,19).

There is, then, strong support in tradition and the Bible for a loving, accepting and encouraging attitude toward even unrepentant sinners. Like Ben, however, some people may find it difficult not to feel judgmental concerning a particular divorce. Although he strongly believes in forgiveness and tries hard not to judge others, his strong feelings currently hold sway.

Interestingly enough, Carl Rogers, a leading proponent of the view that encouragement is a key to a person's progress, does not advocate covering up negative feelings:

> Experience drove home the fact that to act consistently acceptant, for example, if in fact I was

feeling annoyed or skeptical or some other non-acceptant feeling, was certain in the long run to be perceived as inconsistent or untrustworthy. I have come to recognize that being trustworthy does not demand that I be rigidly consistent but that I be dependably real (*On Becoming a Person*, p. 50).

Christians are called upon to recognize their own failings and not look down on the failings of others. As Jesus asked, "How dare you say to your brother, 'Let me take that splinter out of your eye,' when, look, there is a great log in your own?" (Mt 7:3-4). The gospels challenge us to treat others with compassion and understanding.

James Young tells us, "The reason we need to forgive those who have injured us is because we have been forgiven ourselves." Moreover, forgiveness of others is the only way to escape the deforming effects that anger and hatred wreak on their host. Young tells the story of a woman whose husband had left her for another woman 22 years ago. She came to realize: "I was tied up in knots of bitterness and anger. I didn't realize how sour I had become." Inspired to forgiveness while in prayer, she discovered:

> The burden of the past seemed to be lifted off my shoulders. Over the coming months I began to find new energy for myself and my kids. He hasn't been any easier to relate to, but I feel differently toward him, more patient, more understanding. He still bugs me at times, but he can't upset me the way he could before I'd forgiven him (*Divorcing, Believing, Belonging*, New York: Paulist Press, 1984, p. 110).

As Young emphasizes, forgiveness may not seem to affect the other:

> Forgiving former spouses who have injured us doesn't mean blotting out what they have done or even adopting a permissive attitude toward them. Our forgiveness doesn't make them different persons. The most painful aspect of such forgiveness may be that it may not be reciprocated— there may be no sign that a former spouse has forgiven us or looks at us differently. We don't forgive to win forgiveness in return, but rather to move closer to God who is all-forgiving (p. 112).

Forgiveness does not mean being unaware of evil, or of condoning it because ''everyone does it,'' or even in the spirit of one venal official winking at a fellow's bribe-taking. Rather, it is a deep compassion based upon our struggles with our own shortcomings.

Implied in this is the need to change ourselves, to deepen our own understanding. St. Paul wrote movingly of the deep inner struggle that divides the inner life of all human beings:

> Though the will to do what is good is in me, the power to do it is not. The good thing I want to do, I never do; the evil thing I do not want—that is what I do (Rom 7:18-19).

In the suffering that his continual failings bring, he cries out:

> What a wretched man I am! Who will rescue me from this body doomed to death? God—thanks be to him—through Christ Jesus our Lord (Rom 7:24-25).

The more we grow ourselves, by truly feeling how hard the struggle for perfection is, and by growing closer to the compassionate God, the more we can sympathize with someone who seems to be a blatant sinner. We do not overlook evil, any more than Jesus did. But our primary concern will be for the person.

It may be helpful at this point to describe the divorce process, to help create an understanding ''from the inside'' of what the typical divorcing person is going through. We will also touch on various ways in which others have contributed to the weaving of the divorcing person's tapestry and are now participating in its partial unraveling and re-weaving. This may help you begin to work out some of these issues of self-understanding and acceptance. Keep in mind that a deep knowledge of ourselves and of others is the work, study and prayer of a lifetime.

6

The Divorce Process

Divorced people can be difficult to reach. They may pretend nothing is wrong and refuse to talk about their situation; they may talk incessantly about their troubles; they may launch into angry denunciations of their ex-spouses. They may act stunned, or they may pounce upon your most innocent gesture or choice of words. They may refuse to listen to any advice, or they may look to you for minute direction. Often they will shift behavior, sometimes rapidly and drastically.

Understanding what divorcing people go through will help you to understand their sometimes erratic and difficult behavior, and to be more effective in helping them. It will also help you define and deal with your own ideas and feelings about divorce.

A word of caution: It is impossible to draw up a detailed timetable that will fit everyone. Divorce is a complex process that engages one's deepest values and emotions; people and situations vary widely. Nor is divorce a steady, linear process. Especially in the early months, the divorcing person's moods and behavior are likely to swing back and forth dramatically. Nonetheless, we believe that the following generalized account, based upon both research and personal counselling experience, will provide some valuable insights.

Typically, it takes a couple about five years to work through a divorce and establish new identities. The first

14 months are the most intense. During this time, the couple experience the death of their relationship and go through a period of mourning. As time passes and their emotions begin to subside, they launch into new growth.

We have already discussed the gradual death of a relationship in the account of how Jack and Bev built a wall between themselves. Since this book is primarily concerned with those going through a divorce, rather than with marriage counselling, we will concentrate on the stages following the decision to divorce.

During the first 14 months, the divorcing persons focus on their broken relationship and on the void it has left in their lives. The break is typically followed by a shock period, during which they show very little of what they are thinking or feeling.

This is followed by a period in which they erupt with a variety of feelings directed against their ex-partners: helplessness, anger, weeping—all expressions of an underlying desire to regain their earlier, stable environment. During this stage, they commonly lash out at everyone.

As they finally come to realize on a deeper level (not just intellectually) that their marriage has ended, they feel loss and despair, which they may express through restlessness, withdrawal, apathy or even last-ditch attempts to re-establish their old relationship.

After going through this period of despair, they are ready to begin forming new relationships and building their new, separate lives. By this time, they are also able to view their ex-partners more realistically.

You will find that their changing behaviors appear far less disconnected and difficult to understand if you view their actions as varied attempts to deal with their two central problems: loneliness and overload. We will devote the rest of this chapter to loneliness and take up overload in the next chapter.

Loneliness

The divorced feel doubly lonely. Externally, their social tapestry is unraveling: They have lost their most intimate relationship (compounded by the loss of many friends and in-laws), and their ''divorced'' status frequently seems to disrupt their broader community relations. Internally, they typically react to actual and imagined slights by withdrawing from others:

> . . . like the cat that sits down on a hot stove lid. She will never sit down on a hot stove lid again—and that is well; but also she will never sit down on a cold one any more (Mark Twain, ''Pudd'nhead Wilson's New Calendar,'' in *Following the Equator*).

Divorced people usually feel openly rejected by their ex-spouses, either because the latter instigated the divorce or because they experienced the latter's ''bricks.'' Others may openly express rejection, like the ushers who asked Betty and her children not to bring up the gifts in church any more.

In most cases, however, divorced people suffer more from being ignored than from being openly rejected. Sally, for example, found herself sitting in the back of church, week after week, as the congregation prayed for the victims of tornados and earthquakes, farmers battered by drought and falling prices for their crops, people suffering from wars in the Far East and so on. As she joined in the prayers for these remote sufferers, she often found herself worrying about how she would survive with her two teen-age daughters, now that she was divorced. She wondered when the congregation would pray for her or for people in broken relationships. She felt invisible, like a non-person whom everyone in the room passed by without noticing.

When she moved, her new community included prayers for people in broken relationships. This simple expression of concern encouraged her to get out of the house with her children. Her present church community gave her the extra emotional energy she needed to continue her life.

Filling in the Void

Pulling back from others is a natural reaction to pain. Like the cat who sat on a hot stove lid, people in the early stages of divorce are on the alert for new dangers. They are highly sensitive to subtle manifestations of rejection in others, and fearful of venturing into new relationships of any kind.

Their withdrawal often appears excessive, like the cat's avoidance of cold stove lids. Especially in the beginning, however, the withdrawal can serve a positive purpose: It creates a space for the one in pain to begin the process of healing. Just as physical injuries take time to heal, so, too, do the emotional injuries suffered in divorce.

Early in the divorce process, the partners miss many small, positive things (and sometimes even the negative ones) that they shared. Many try to fill in the void with ceaseless activity. Some devote long hours to their jobs; others strive to be super moms or dads; still others drug themselves with television. One client went out every night for two years.

Initially, as the divorced seek a little space and time to heal their wounds, such activities might serve a positive end. Done to excess, however, used as an escape from facing their situation and taking positive action, such frantic activities could prove harmful.

A major way of helping the divorced deal with loneliness is to step into the void created by their divorce and withdrawal. Especially in the beginning, it is important to do this in a gentle, caring way. Because of their fear and hypersensitivity, the newly divorced easily overload emotionally. However well-intentioned, pushing them too quickly may cause them to withdraw even more.

At the same time, being ignored is one of their greatest sources of pain, for it intensifies their feeling of rejection and plants or nourishes inner doubt and feelings of guilt. Making yourself available to divorced people when needed is most helpful. Even though we sometimes fail to say what they want to hear, the fact of being physically present, caring about them and not judging them makes a difference.

Those who live at a distance can offer their presence through a telephone call, a card or a letter. These approaches can also be used by those who live closer, during periods when the divorced do not feel up to going out or having visitors. The message can be as simple as "I miss you." Simply knowing that one is being thought about can be a comfort.

The psychology of "availability" can be seen in the typical behavior of young children. So long as the parent is at hand, they may be content to play by themselves and may even reject direct attention as an interruption. However, a telephone call or a visitor may trigger a series of attention-getting shenanigans, because they sense that the parent, though physically present, is no longer available to them—they have become "invisible" to the parent.

It is important to the divorced to maintain and even strengthen their bonds with relatives and friends, and to gradually reach out and create new friendships. Helping them maintain old ties limits the damage to their existing tapestry; helping them weave new friendships and interests fills in the bare spots left by the rended scenes.

You can help them do this by continuing to invite them to customary affairs with family members or old

friends, and by getting them to join church groups, perhaps even a church-sponsored divorce group. The key
factor, especially in the beginning, is to get them into
gatherings where they can mingle without feeling pres-
sured or judged. Again, common sense must be your
guide to avoid pushing them too fast.

A client once told how she had made herself available to a neighbor who was struggling with a divorce.
Joyce was 57 years old and had been widowed for five
years when her young next-door neighbors, Bill and
Laura, divorced each other. Bill moved out and Laura
stayed behind with their three children.

During the first months, Laura stayed in the house
most of the time, and both her children and her house
showed neglect. Joyce could see that Laura needed help,
but didn't know any direct ways of helping her or even of
talking about her problems. Instead, when Laura came
outside during the first months, Joyce would simply
make small talk with her. As time passed, Laura began
talking about her pain, especially her loneliness. At first,
Joyce mainly listened. After Laura had gradually filled in
her story, Joyce began talking a little about her own pain
and loneliness following her husband's death. After a
time, Laura began to notice how they shared many of the
same emotions.

Joyce also offered help in little, unobtrusive ways.
Whenever she went shopping, she stopped by to ask if
Laura needed anything at the store. When Laura and the
children seemed especially down, Joyce would take a
plate of cookies over to them.

One day, it occurred to Joyce that Laura never got
out. Knowing that Bill took the children every other
weekend, Joyce invited Laura out for coffee her next
"free" Saturday. This Saturday coffee became a bi-
monthly ritual.

Slowly, Laura began changing. She smiled more often and showed renewed self-confidence. As she talked about her divorce, she dwelt less on the past and began talking more about future plans. When she did talk about Bill, she expressed markedly less bitterness. Two years after the divorce, Laura had found a job and was taking better care of her house, her children and herself. Best of all, the children had settled down as well.

When asked what special things she had done to help Laura, Joyce smiled and said that it was just little things, like showing concern and making herself available. Tears came into her eyes as she added, ''It was like in my old neighborhood when my husband died. A person from my church did the same thing for me, and I felt that I should pass it on to someone else who was hurting.''

Joyce's sustained care helped Laura re-establish a sense of self-worth. That, in turn, gave her the confidence to tackle her expanded responsibilities. Having an acquaintance become an important friend began a trend toward reweaving the damaged tapestry and demonstrated that not all stove lids are hot. Doing things, even something so modest as going out for coffee, gave Laura some sense of control over her life, a feeling that she could effect changes for the better.

Laura's gradual realization that Joyce had gone through similar suffering and shared the problem of loneliness marked an important development: a change from focusing on her own problems to focusing outward. This outward focusing is the key difference between being lonely and being alone. Imagine a room with many windows: one person enters, closes the door, and begins gazing out of a window. Whatever the view—crowded city streets or quiet country scenes—this person finds much of interest in the real world. This person is alone, but is not truly lonely.

Imagine a different type of person alone in this room, one for whom the windows act as mirrors. Here the focus is always inward, back on the self. The real world seems not to exist. This sense of isolation makes a person truly lonely.

By helping the divorced deal with external loneliness, encouraging them to focus outward and feel more confident, you will also help them deal with internal loneliness, a reality that must ultimately be dealt with by the divorced themselves. Making yourself available, helping them to maintain and expand their social ties, and offering continual encouragement are the water and fertilizer that nurture growth. After doing your best, all that is left is to watch and pray that the seed will grow.

Two means that are most helpful in conquering loneliness are prayer and humor, which we will take up in connection with anger. First, though, we will examine the broader subject of emotional overload, of which anger is generally the chief symptom.

7

Overload

One of the most difficult things for the newly divorced to deal with is the flood of emotions. Even during their best moments, their emotions are raw, close to the surface. This makes them feel unable to handle even routine problems; the ordinary ups and downs of daily life tend to become crises. Their fragility is punctuated with frequent tears, which may be triggered by looking at a flower or a picture, hearing a chance remark or being asked to do something.

The divorced often feel both task and emotional overload. Task overload is having too many things to do—not only doing what the ex-spouse used to take care of, but often having to handle many affairs in connection with the divorce proceedings. Emotional overload occurs when a person has to give and give with no end in sight, such as the single parent of five or six kids. This person may also be looking for extra personal attention because of the insecurity that he or she may feel over the divorce.

Even those not going through a crisis such as divorce can feel overwhelmed by daily events. Imagine a person coming home from work feeling very tired. He sifts through the mail for a friendly letter but finds several bills instead. Next he discovers that one of the kids is sick and the others are fighting. For the *coup de grace*, the cat has diarrhea and someone has unplugged the refrigerator. What is there left to do but sit down and cry or yell a lot?

A flood of emotions is a normal response in critical situations. Seeing your divorced friend or relative going through this is, in itself, no cause for becoming overly disturbed. Moreover, you can suggest some general measures that will help them.

Telling Their Story

Recently, two truck drivers were conversing via CB radios as they drove across Texas. The first one related that he had not been feeling well for the past four months even though there did not appear to be anything physically wrong with him. Later on, he revealed that he had been divorced four months earlier. At the end of the conversation, he remarked that he was feeling a bit better. The second driver had been helpful simply by listening to the story and not being judgmental.

In part, listening shows your interest; it demonstrates that your divorced friend or relative is still important to you. In larger part, though, listening helps them to take a significant step toward gaining emotional control: telling their story.

Because their situation seems to them catastrophic and overwhelming, they tend to focus all of their energy and attention on the divorce and block out everything else. Seeing only problems that they feel unable to overcome, they experience feelings of inadequacy washing over them.

Paradoxically, despite the large amount of time spent dwelling on their plight, they also may block out many of the realities that led to the divorce. Because their emotions run so high, they find it painful to dwell on many aspects of the divorce. Often they feel unable to acknowledge their own responsibility for what happened. A participant in one divorce group complained that her life had been ruined by her former husband. Later on, it came out that she had been divorced for over 29 years. At times dwelling on one's role as a victim of another's actions can exonerate one from taking any positive, restorative action.

By telling the whole story of the divorce, they can finally see what has happened to them in an organized way. This enables them to put their situation within boundaries. If both you and they feel up to it, you might encourage them to tell you about it, or you might suggest that they see a counsellor about it. Getting them to join a discussion group comprised of divorced people can be even more beneficial. If they choose not to tell everything to another person, they should at least write it out for themselves. The important thing is that they get their whole story out where they can eventually deal with it more objectively.

Taking Control of Their Lives

As we have said, it takes about five years to go through a divorce and establish a new way of life. Because emotional adjustments take time, we have cautioned against overloading the divorced with invitations that they are not ready to handle.

Nevertheless, this does not mean that the divorced should simply lie around and wait for things to improve. Divorce is a crisis that must be dealt with here and now. In any crisis, the inevitable sense of a loss of control escalates the problem. For example, Diane felt overwhelmed not only by having to take full charge of her home and her child, but even more by having to find her first job without any relevant experience or even a high-school diploma.

Natural reactions to a loss of control are expressions of anger and blaming, weeping and seeking commiseration, withdrawing into passivity. Diane gave in to depression by staying in bed most of each day. Although these actions may create some time and space for the emotions to subside, they do not attack the root problem of control, because they do nothing to relieve the practical difficulties that are weighing one down.

The best solution lies in taking action, even in seemingly trivial matters. In *Control Theory*, William Glasser relates that a friend of his who owns a business in a highly competitive field often has to cope with unexpected problems such as bad weather, supplier strikes and rapidly changing government regulations. When these gang up on him, he feels as though he is losing control of the whole operation. His way of overcoming his panic and regaining a sense of control during these crises is to go to a supermarket and buy some special treats:

> He feels better with each item he tosses in his basket. By the time he gets home, his mind is so filled with pictures of ice cream topped with raspberries or blueberries that the troubles of the office seem to melt away.

Why is this effective?

> Regardless of how we *feel*, we always have some control over what we *do*. When my friend loses control, he goes food shopping. If nowhere else, in the market he is in command (*Control Theory*, Harper Perennial Library edition, 1985, p. 45).

In the beginning, small, easy, even trivial-seeming activities can prove to be powerful in breaking up the emotional log jam. You might encourage the person to express an opinion on a subject or open a bank account in his or her own name. Even the smallest step in restructuring their lives gives them a sense of direction, of being in control.

You might also advise them to make a list of things to be done and then to number the items in the order of their importance. Not everything needs to be done at once, for they have a limited amount of energy. The most important thing is that they simply start at the top and begin to act on their needs.

The natural resources of family and friends can help for a short time—for example, someone might offer to baby-sit so they can handle an important task or enjoy a short respite from constant parenting.

Positive Challenges

Encouraging the divorced to take positive action should not be confused with impatiently exhorting them to ''get off their duff.'' This kind of criticism can be highly destructive, in that it tends to reinforce their feelings of guilt and inadequacy. Divorced persons often feel that they ought to live up to certain standards. Being divorced and feeling that others look down upon them because of it makes them feel second-class; their inner hurt over this increases their self-consciousness.

Being overly sympathetic, however, can also be harmful. The recipient of too much sympathy may interpret your intentions in the way Sidney Harris did when he argued: ''We always have a slight feeling of superiority when someone else suffers a tragedy, and it makes us feel good to feel bad about it.'' Or, at best, if there is no smugness involved, there may be some self-concern mixed in:

> It takes no great moral or spiritual qualities to feel sorry for a person who has fallen from a tremendous height, or has suffered an irreplaceable loss. We can easily put ourselves in his place, and feel sorrow for ourselves, in a vicarious fashion (''But Can You Sympathize with Joy?'', in *The Best of Sydney J. Harris*, Boston: Houghton Mifflin, 1975, p. 4).

Harris deprecates not genuine compassion but pity. Although pity has generally been considered a humane attitude, *Webster's New Dictionary of Synonyms* notes a possible darker side:

> Pity sometimes may suggest a tinge of contempt for one who is inferior whether because of suffering or from inherent weakness; there is also a frequent suggestion that the effect if not the purpose of pity is to keep the object in a weak or inferior state.

We recommend genuine, feeling-level involvement with others as equals. This means recognizing both their difficulties and their capabilities and being concerned not that they keep certain rules or conform to certain standards but that they realize their God-given potential.

Such loving concern can help fill in the gap left by the loss of their spouse and many friends. According to Father John Powell, genuine love has three attributes: one, I am on your side; two, I know that you have the qualities to do what you have to do; and three, I will challenge you to act on these qualities. Again, the challenge is not so much "oughts" as general encouragement to discover their true selves. As they do so, they will regain control of their lives and build up the self-esteem they need to cope.

Anger

Anger, whether one's own or another's, is difficult to deal with, especially in its aggressive forms—yelling, throwing things, even physically attacking another. Anger usually causes others to feel threatened, while the person experiencing the anger feels out of control or even evil. Because of this double-edged threat, anger is commonly regarded as anti-social, and many people suppress its more aggressive expressions, only to have it break out in many other ways. However it is manifested, it tends to isolate its subject.

In dealing with the divorcing, you will often be confronted with their anger. If you continue to make yourself available and demonstrate your acceptance of them while they are struggling with their anger, you will prove immeasurably helpful to them.

This chapter begins by showing ways in which the divorced typically express their anger. It then looks at this emotion more closely and suggests ways of feeling more comfortable with it. In the next chapter, we will suggest ways of dealing with some of the more common, and difficult, behaviors through which the divorcing express their anger.

Because anger plays a prominent part in the divorce process, support groups often devote several sessions to understanding it and searching for ways to turn it to positive uses. One group focused on the myriad ways in which they expressed their anger. Because they shared the same predicament and had gotten to know and care about each other, they were able to penetrate their outward differences to the shared underlying emotions.

Anger and one's defenses are intensified by the divorce experience. People often feel vulnerable with other people and therefore use their anger to maintain a "safe" distance. This is an underlying characteristic in each of the following examples.

The group's reactions provide an index of how well each member was coping with anger: They treated those who were still immersed in more subjective struggles with quiet acceptance or gentle reassurance; they responded with direct advice or even some humor to those who had objectified their anger enough to understand it. Humor, as we shall see in greater detail, is an important way of objectifying, and thereby mastering, anger.

Alice, a dental hygienist, described most of her anger as overload. When she was overwhelmed, she could feel her body getting sick, and her face would become flushed; in extremely bad times, she would break out with skin problems. The group listened carefully but allowed her the distance she needed.

Jack, a businessman, found that his anger went through two stages. As the anger first gripped him, he released emotional energy by yelling. After blowing off some steam and becoming aware of his own and others' agitation, he started worrying that he was out of control. To avoid further embarrassment, he turned to the second stage: working off some of his energy by doing all kinds of jobs at work and at home. Several in the group quipped that he was welcome to come to their homes the next time he needed to work off some energy. The group enjoyed a good laugh over this.

Fred, a lawyer, enjoyed performing in front of people. The courtroom afforded him an ideal arena in which to work off his anger; he used lots of body language there, including a red face, clenched fist, and pounding on the table. Many in the group noted that their lawyers had acted similarly in court; some thought the pattern fitted their ex-partners. One member got a good laugh by remarking that, for $150 an hour for court time, Fred *should* put on a good performance. Mixed in with the humor was some bitterness about their lawyers in the divorce process.

Sally, a secretary, had a quick sense of humor. She explained that the angrier she felt, the more hostile her humor became. This increased her discomfort, for she did not want to hurt others. The group sensed her underlying good nature and showed that they genuinely liked her.

Jessica, a doctor, enjoyed exercising her considerable talents in a number of areas. Displaying competency became an important prop to her self-esteem as her marriage collapsed. However, when dealing with matters she felt less secure about, she used blaming to keep other people away. She realized that a little blaming afforded her some room for healing, but she tended to get stuck in her blaming mode. Because of this, she felt that others thought she was cold, which in turn increased her sense of vulnerability and her defensive blaming. Several men in the group said they had fallen into the same trap.

Mark, a policeman, came across as a very nice guy. In describing his work, he related how he became forgetful and frequently lost things while he was going through his divorce. By always coming late to work, he set himself up to be reprimanded. Because he felt bored most of the time, he found himself continually interrupting others, which naturally provoked them to express irritation or to avoid talking with him. A fellow officer had confronted him about these behaviors, commenting that Mark seemed very angry.

Diane, a housewife, was mostly down on herself. She said she hated herself when her anger flared up, so she often had a drink to quell these feelings. To deal with her alcoholism, she was seeing another counselor. The two people sitting on either side of her touched her to offer their reassurance.

Jim, who was unemployed, tended to work out his anger by picking arguments and throwing things. He had kept things stirred up most of the time while his marriage was disintegrating. In retrospect, he concluded that his underlying motive had been to prevent others from focusing on him.

At present, he spends many an hour throwing stones into a nearby lake. He finds this setting restful, and throwing stones is a far cheaper form of therapy than throwing things at home. He has also worked out a method of regaining control of himself by taking a deep breath and blowing it out slowly, then repeating this sequence nine times.

Michelle, a salesperson, found herself talking more as her anger mounted. Although this made her feel better for the moment, it often got her into trouble, especially when she leaked confidential information. To overcome this habit, she was trying to listen more.

Sam, a construction worker, could not seem to find his anger. Typically, he laughed a lot and habitually smiled at his three small children. Even on the rare occasions when he became upset with them, he did not lose his temper, though he tended to eat a lot more. Mark, the policeman, suggested that he was stuffing his feelings, a view that Sam found insightful.

Cora, a nurse, escaped from anger or other disturbing emotions by daydreaming. She worried, however, that this could lead to more trouble, especially when she was working in the hospital. Alice, the dental hygienist, suggested that the next time Cora caught herself daydreaming, she bring herself back to reality by asking herself why she was angry.

George, a mechanic, was very quiet. With some diffidence, he asked whether others in the group had ever culminated an argument with their ex-partners by going to bed with them. This experience left him feeling as though he and his ex-wife had made up. Sally and Fred said they had done the same thing with their ex-partners.

Even this modest-sized group displays wide differences in ways of expressing anger—from Jim's yelling and picking fights to Cora's daydreaming and Sam's apparent calmness and overeating. The more aggressive forms of anger are sometimes directed against others, such as Jim's picking fights and Jessica's criticizing, and sometimes directed against the self, such as Mark's setting himself up to be criticized. Some anger is destructive, like Diane's immobility and alcoholism, and some is turned to more constructive ends, such as Jack's work, Fred's courtroom tirades on behalf of his clients and Sam's interactions with his children.

After discussing their individual cases, the group delved into the common factors underlying their varied manifestations of anger. Expressing anger is generally viewed as unpleasant and destructive. Consequently, after expressing anger, people typically feel silly, embarrassed or remorseful, and are often punished for it by others' reactions.

Trying to control expressions of anger without understanding the emotion itself, however, often leads people to adopt one or more of the following attitudes or behaviors:

Debt: Thankfulness and anger do not go together—"I can't get angry with a person who has been so nice to me." The person suppressing anger out of an unhealthy sense of debt reacts out of a fear that he or she is being selfish and ungrateful. On the other hand, one might be angry with another and still feel obliged to give that person gifts and attention for fear that refusing to do so will signal that something is wrong in the relationship. This person is afraid that the other will break off the relationship. The insidious danger in this tactic is that the other may sense that affection is being bought or that the giver has no sense of self-worth, and so come to feel contempt for the giver.

Fear of losing control: The feeling of being swept along by anger can make people think they are going crazy. To maintain a feeling of control, they suppress their anger. Although they may succeed for a time, the anger continues fermenting inside and will suddenly burst forth with explosive force. This creates a vicious circle, in that the explosion seems more like insanity than a normal burst of anger, and so drives them to try even harder to suppress their anger.

This is especially strong in those who have not learned when and how to say no. They have an image of always agreeing with others. Eventually, resentment builds up to a sudden outburst of anger that catches others completely by surprise; the puzzled reactions reinforce the person's own impression that the outburst was irrational and therefore bordering on craziness.

Fear of repeating their parents' errors: People who witnessed violent conflicts between their parents fear that they will develop the same faults. This fear is intensified in those who had violent confrontations with their parents.

Guilt or fear of retaliation: Society or parents had inculcated several of the group with the idea that anger is bad. As children, they learned to avoid expressing anger because it exposed them to ridicule, punishment, feelings of guilt and warnings about offending God. As adults, many had experienced retaliation for their expressions of anger—being yelled at, ridiculed before others, given the silent treatment or even attacked physically.

Respectability: Some felt the need to look good at all times by keeping their cool. This was especially true of professional people and those with high profile positions in the community.

The unsettling effects of anger make this feeling seem socially and psychologically undesirable. As we have said repeatedly, acceptance is the key to helping the divorcing, and that means accepting anger. Begin by accepting your own anger, because those who are uncomfortable with their own anger will hardly feel comfortable with another's.

Anger is an inborn trait. From the moment it takes its first breath, a baby is capable of expressing anger in unmistakable ways; in contrast, it takes months to learn even a rudimentary form of humor, and years to love on a deep level. Such a natural, universal emotion is an inevitable part of human nature, so accepting it is a necessary part of truly accepting human nature.

Since human nature is essentially good, an inherent trait like anger must have a good purpose. In its basic form, anger is a call to overcome an obstacle to something one needs or to ward off something harmful. The baby who lies passively is more likely to remain hungry or soiled than one who vents his frustration with loud cries. The toddler who fights against excessive restrictions will learn and become independent faster than one who submits out of fear or discouragement.

Similarly, anger is an important driving force for many divorced people. As the tapestry of their life unravels, they snatch it from others in order to protect it from further damage. Directing anger at another also helps divert their attention from the damage, lest they despair at what they see and chuck the whole thing. It becomes a temporary way of maintaining some kind of belief in and control over themselves and their tapestry.

In the beginning, anger can help them distance themselves from others. It can keep them from having to face their own faults before they can handle them. It can also spur them to action. Those who crumple in mute despair are in a far more precarious state than those who occasionally rant and rage. It took Diane over two and a half years to build up the energy to find a satisfying job; the openly angry, in contrast, already have abundant energy, which simply needs to be diverted into productive channels.

Although the view that anger is unacceptable would seem to be reinforced by Christian religions, another sign that anger has its good side is the fact that the Bible frequently ascribes it to God. In the Old Testament, God frequently expresses anger over the people turning to false gods or oppressing the weak. The purpose of God's anger and punishments, though, is not blind vengeance, but the return of the people to God's love and to justice toward others.

We often think of Jesus as unfailingly gentle. Charity, or love, is the ultimate meaning of Christianity, and Jesus praised the meek in the Sermon on the Mount. We may recall his mild, sad reproaches to his betrayer, Judas, or his quiet acceptance of insults, false conviction, torture and painful, ignominious death. But the Bible also recounts several occasions on which he expressed anger.

Typically he conveyed his anger through words and firm opposition. The Pharisees were his major targets, for in professing to follow God's law they were actually seeking acclaim for themselves; worse, they attacked the spirit of God in rejecting the healings of Jesus and laid oppressive requirements on others, thus driving people away from God's love.

The extended indictment of the scribes and Pharisees in chapter 23 of Matthew's gospel blazes with anger:

They tie up heavy burdens and lay them on people's shoulders, but will they lift a finger to move them? Not they! Everything they do is done to attract attention, like wearing broader headbands and longer tassels, like wanting to take the place of honor at banquets and the front seats in the synagogues, being greeted respectfully in the market squares and having people call them Rabbi. . . .

Alas for you, scribes and Pharisees, you hypocrites! You who shut up the kingdom of Heaven in people's faces, neither going in yourselves nor allowing others to go in who want to.

Alas for you, scribes and Pharisees, you hypocrites! You who travel over sea and land to make a single proselyte, and anyone who becomes one you make twice as fit for hell as you are (Mt 23:4-7, 13-15).

All four gospels relate how Jesus drove the money-changers and merchants from the Temple. We can imagine how this came to pass. Typically, Jesus sought quiet and solitude in which to pray. He chose the wilderness, whose sparse vegetation and mountains bespoke a vast emptiness that simultaneously showed God's raw power and made the beholder ache for God's fulfilling presence. Yet he was also strongly drawn to his Father's house, the Temple in Jerusalem. We can be sure that he also prayed there.

Imagine, then, how the buying and selling must have disrupted quiet prayer or earnest discussion. The caged pigeons, unable to escape the cruel sun; the tethered sheep and cattle that continuously brayed out their unremitting discomfort. The sellers added raucous offers of their wares and impassioned haggling over quality and prices. The turmoil was made more oppressive by the stench of the animals and their droppings, and the annoying flies they attracted.

Worse than the turmoil was the unhallowed spirit of many sellers and buyers alike. Some sellers greedily took advantage of pilgrims unfamiliar with local prices and money, and attempted to foist blemished animals upon unknowledgeable buyers, though offering such animals clearly violated both the letter and the spirit of the Law. Some shrewd buyers, aware of the generally higher quality of the animals, shopped there for their own tables, thus turning the Temple into a butcher shop.

Such disruptiveness and open scandal in this holy place stirred deep anger in Jesus. His daily teachings about loving God and turning away from material concerns were ignored by those whose habits and profits kept them returning day after day. Only direct action would bring about a change. The gospels show us that Jesus did act:

> When the time of the Jewish Passover was near Jesus went up to Jerusalem, and in the Temple he found people selling cattle and sheep and doves, and the money changers sitting there. Making a whip out of cord, he drove them all out of the Temple, sheep and cattle as well, scattered the money changers' coins, knocked their tables over and said to the dove sellers, ''Take all this out of here and stop using my Father's house as a market.'' Then his disciples remembered the words of scripture: I am eaten up with zeal for your house (Jn 2:13-19).

In the synoptic gospels, Jesus states his motive clearly: ''Does not Scripture say, *My house will be called a house of prayer for all the peoples*? But you have turned it into *a bandits' den*'' (Mk 19:17).

In the next chapter, we will suggest ways of helping the divorced convert their anger into the energy they need to restructure their lives.

9

Dealing
With Anger

Anger is a call to action. When we feel frustrated or oppressed, anger can rouse us to correct this condition. Because the feeling runs deep and the need is real we must act. Suppressing the emotion, far from solving the problem, creates a growing pressure that will eventually break us down or explode with destructive force against others.

The danger involved with anger is that aroused people often direct their anger against the wrong person or in ways that are ineffective or destructive. Aggressive expressions of anger should never be encouraged. According to a number of psychological studies, "letting off steam," whether through direct aggression or through strenuous exercise, seems to increase anger and aggression (Ronald H. Bailey, *Violence and Aggression*, "Human Behavior" series, Time-Life Books, 1976, pp. 145-169).

This presents us with an apparent dilemma: Giving free rein to anger and suppressing it are both destructive. The solution lies in seeing anger as a symptom, a surface emotion that is driven by a deep need. Once you pierce the surface anger, you find deeper feelings—envy, hurt, guilt, need—that people have difficulty dealing with. They escape from these feelings through anger. The feelings are interconnected, a chain of causes and effects—

for instance, detachment, loneliness (lack of feeling love), low self-esteem and finally anger.

Anger brings some benefits to newly divorced people: distance while their wounds heal, time to build up their energy and self-confidence before tackling their problems, and so on. However, anger also entails the pain of isolation and inner turmoil. Eventually, a divorced person has to decide whether the benefits are rewarding enough to continue enduring the pain. This decision may parallel an earlier one of determining whether the benefits of a deteriorating marriage were enough to continue enduring its pains.

Since anger is a call for action, long-standing anger implies that the person does not recognize the possibility of effecting a meaningful change and feels frustrated. It may also be an excuse for refusing to take responsibility for oneself. A decision to deal with anger is a decision to change what you can change and sweep aside those feelings of anger that hold you back.

The following means of dealing with anger can apply to you, the friend or relative of the divorced, since you may have strong feelings about the correctness or rightness of the divorce.

Because anger is natural and often only a surface reaction, you should not become overly concerned about it. For example, do not worry that anger in itself is evil or that it dooms you or the divorced socially. The first step in dealing with anger is to define it: Determine whether you are angry, and, if you are, pinpoint the target of your anger.

Then take steps to calm yourself or whoever is angry. This deals mainly with the physical side of anger, which entails the building up of adrenaline. This results in tension, increased blood pressure and extra energy. Exercise, even something as simple as walking, is an excellent way of working off this excess energy.

Working off anger can also be done with humor. Sara began by breaking dishes, but, finding this to be too expensive, she soon resorted to carrying a tray of ice cubes outside, hurling them onto her back sidewalk, one by one, and then stomping on them. The neighbors thought she was losing it, but this worked for her because she felt the humor of it. Note that if she had earnestly imagined that she was physically attacking her ex-husband, this same exercise would have increased her anger.

Vigorous exercise is a good safety valve for releasing pent-up anger that is threatening to explode. When the anger is less pressing, try the following exercise to move from brokenness to growth via a positive attitude.

First, lie with your back on the floor, your feet slightly apart, and your palms pressed against the floor. Take three or four deep breaths and blow the last one out through your mouth. Close your eyes (30 percent of your emotional energy drains out through them) and try to relax.

Second, allow your strong feelings about the divorce to come forward. Don't fight them; just let them become a part of you.

Third, associate these feelings with a particular situation or locale.

Fourth, try to think of an effective way of dealing with these feelings without harming yourself or others.

Fifth, take another deep breath and, as you slowly blow it out your mouth, imagine that it is a green mist containing your angry feelings.

Finally, imagine yourself back in the situation or locale that you have associated with your anger, but now without your strong feelings; picture yourself handling the situation. Congratulate yourself on acting in a positive way.

As you repeat this exercise, you will find yourself letting go of a little more brokenness in your life. For a divorced person, this could mean moving beyond the pain of the divorce; for a friend or relative, this could mean letting go of judgmental feelings about the divorce.

Working off physical energy calms the body, enabling one to concentrate on the inner spiritual anger. This latter must be dealt with, for it is the source of the physical anger.

Spiritually, you have to confront the actual situation by entering into the feelings as strongly as possible. You may find this to be intense, but it won't hurt you. Focus on those parts of the situation that arouse your strongest feelings. When you have identified those feelings, invite Jesus into the scene. Imagine yourself handing these feelings to him, then stepping back to see what he does with them. This takes faith, for you need to move into a deeper understanding of life's processes. As you do this, you move closer to Jesus. This moves you to forgive, which in turn will bring you further healing.

At this point, you or the divorced person may object, "I'm not sure I feel like forgiving, or that I can." It is important to realize that forgiveness is a decision, not a feeling or an instantaneous, once-and-for-all act. Many movies and television shows have depicted teary-eyed, "Oh, yes! I forgive!" encounters between characters. In real life, people move slowly, step by step: They forgive a little bit here, a little bit there. Instead of saying, "I forgive everything," try forgiving something small, perhaps some minor annoyance, like the person's past habit of leaving things lying around, habitually being five minutes late, snoring or wearing clothes you didn't like.

For each step in dealing with your anger, you will typically have to combine the physical and the spiritual—for example, do some exercise to calm down, then perform the exercise of handing this particular hurt to Jesus. As you continue practicing this, you will get better and better at it. You will also find yourself healing and growing more deeply into your life. In fact, Jesus may be calling you to just this kind of growth.

People respond to divorce on three levels: belief, logic, and emotion. A few generalizations are presented here concerning these mental processes and the way these exercises will touch these areas.

Belief ranges from general expectations about life to trust in another person to religious tenets. People may believe divorce is a legitimate solution to an impossible relationship, or they may decree that a marriage should last for life, regardless of circumstances. Whatever one's own specific positions on divorce, it is important to develop an underlying belief that God still cares, as illustrated in Jesus' parable of the prodigal son.

Logic: They may or may not see divorce as a reasonable solution to a broken relationship. Even if they do not generally accept divorce, they may come to accept this particular instance of it because they cannot find an alternative action.

Emotion may not be connected with belief or logic—those whose beliefs reject divorce may feel relieved that a loved one has escaped from a bad relationship; those who accept divorce in theory may feel shocked or vulnerable over the break-up of what they saw as an ideal marriage.

Anyone thrown into turmoil by these conflicting views may want to talk things through with someone else. Ultimately, it is necessary to integrate these three points of view, so that one's beliefs seem logical and feel right. One comfort is that despite some temporary turmoil one's convictions do prevail in the end.

Remember, all healing takes time. If you broke an arm or a leg, you would quiet yourself down, be gentle with yourself, take better care of yourself and rest the arm or leg.

Blame

Blame is one manifestation of anger and the complex emotions that lie beneath it. People tend to experience hurt as a form of injustice—someone has caused their problem. A person hurt by a divorce tends to point the finger of blame at the ex-partner or others who may have influenced the ex-partner.

During the first three or four months following the break, blaming may help the partners to push others away in order to gain the quiet and privacy they need to begin healing. Should this intense blaming continue for a year or longer, it may mean that they do not want to examine their own shortcomings and begin taking charge of their own lives. Afraid to face their own weakness and guilt and to incur further failures by venturing out into life, they continue a negative relationship. They find this more comfortable than the risk of ending it and having nothing at all—a frightening void.

It is difficult for the divorced to express their anger, and it is uncomfortable to be around people, divorced or not, who constantly rant about others. The best course is to listen to them without becoming caught up in the accusations yourself. If you get tired of listening to the same story, encourage them to write their feelings in a notebook—by pouring out all their feelings, they tend to free themselves to start moving through the next phase of the divorce.

Loving a divorced person does not oblige you to hate or cast blame upon the ex-partner, and certainly does not oblige the friends and relatives of one ex-partner to form an alliance against the other's friends and family. Maintaining friendships with ''the other side'' is personally important to you and them. It may be very important for the children of the divorced couple: The central part of their tapestry has been rent, so keeping the surrounding portions intact gives them stability as well as the hope that their whole world will not be torn asunder.

At first, your refusal to join in the recriminations may provoke irritation in your divorced relative or friend. In the long run, though, your steadfastness in listening and offering help should prevail in showing your concern, and should convince the divorced that you are still "on their side" even though you do not join with them in attacking the ex-partner. Your objectivity can help the divorced to break out of their self-centered gloom by seeing beyond their own needs, recognizing good in others and gaining a more even perspective.

By letting the divorced talk out their anger and blaming and by discussing the matters with them, you significantly further the healing process. If the intense blaming extends beyond a year, however, they may need to see a counsellor.

Similar advice applies to you. Those connected with the divorced may also use blaming as a distancing tactic, to avoid confronting deeper problems. You can help yourself by discussing your anger with good friends, a professional counsellor or a priest or minister.

In dealing with anger and blaming, the important thing is finally to take charge of one's life and move on.

Robbin found herself seething with energy when she was first divorced. She told her divorce group that she felt like a boiling pot: lift the lid even slightly and all the steam pours out uncontrollably. She decided to use some of this energy in a positive way and try to spend less time blaming her ex-partner.

The following week, she reported that she had scrubbed her entire basement floor. The group agreed that this was a good way to work off her energy. The following week was so bad that she scrubbed the basement floor three times. She commented that she could have eaten off it without misgivings. After a number of weeks, she grew tired of scrubbing, so the group brainstormed to come up with alternative outlets for her energy.

She finally decided to channel her efforts into her profession. As a grade-school teacher she was used to speaking to her classes, but she was terrified of speaking before groups of adults. The divorce group helped her set up a system of building her self-confidence in preparation for public speaking. The simple method was stroking herself five times a day after doing normal tasks. For example, after brushing her hair, she would tell herself, "Robbin, you did a good job." This helped build up her self-esteem.

After several months of this, Robbin decided to test herself by persuading the school board to support an important project. She put together a seven-minute presentation, carefully accumulating her facts and stroking herself as she went along: "That's a good argument"; "This statistic will anchor my argument here"; "This practice went well."

Still, as the time for her presentation drew near, she felt increasingly nervous. She felt reassured when told that a certain amount of excitement is not only normal but necessary to get her adrenaline flowing, to perform well and convey enthusiasm to the audience. Afterward, she reported that she had been congratulated by the board and the two teachers who had accompanied her for moral support.

Taking charge of one's life in new endeavors is often easier than dealing with the wounds of the past. But ultimately it is important to apply this take-charge attitude toward the divorce itself.

After Jack and Bev's marriage had died, Bev grew fearful about her economic security. She remembered her childhood, when her parents had never had enough money. Having spent most of her adult life caring for the home, she had little confidence about finding a decent-paying job. Although Jack agreed to pay support for her and the children, fear and anger soon spurred the ex-partners into disagreements.

Matters grew worse when Bev hired a lawyer. At first, Jack and Bev met with him to work out an agreement but the lawyer objected that he could only represent one party so Jack hired his own lawyer. This did not bring them any closer to an agreement because the two lawyers continued arguing over the same issues. All that Jack and Bev had to show for their efforts were over $20,000 in legal fees.

At last the realization that they were getting poorer moved them to break out of their debilitating pattern of fear and anger. Jack called and asked Bev to meet him at a neutral spot, a bench in a small park near their home. There he suggested that they either try again to work out the agreements by themselves or hire a mediator. Bev asked for two days to get her feelings under control and think about it, after which she agreed to give it a try.

They went to a mediator, who helped them devise a property settlement that allowed both of them to part with dignity. After having their lawyers check the agreement, they submitted it in court. The judge seemed happy to find two partners who had assumed their responsibilities in an adult manner.

After the divorce, they took a two-pronged approach to working out their remaining shared responsibilities, primarily their parental duties.

For dealing with their personal feelings, they sought outside help. Jack joined a divorce group, one of the many groups in the United States and Canada run by organizations such as Beginning Experience or the North American Conference of Separated and Divorced Catholics. Bev opted for personal counselling. Their sessions helped each of them to walk through their brokenness and grow as adults.

They agreed to discuss continuing questions regarding their children in a businesslike way and to keep their personal disagreements out of it. They did this by having coffee once a month at a neutral spot. Their rules were to talk only about the children, and to treat each other as they themselves would like to be treated. There were days when one or the other had to call an emotional ''time out'' but for the most part they succeeded in cooperating over the children—they continued to act as parents and helped their children feel loved by both of them.

Once Jack and Bev saw their efforts succeeding, they found it increasingly easy to move on to new ventures. In part, the success itself encouraged them. But more importantly they focused on each other as contributors to the successes rather than as sources of problems and bad feelings.

In order to work together, they had to be on their best behavior, especially in the beginning. Whatever emotional problems they experienced they mainly worked out separately—Jack with his divorce group and Bev with her counsellor, although they would occasionally lose control and become upset with each other.

As part of their businesslike approach, they were direct and honest with each other; as a result they started to get along better. They could cooperate in parenting even though their personal relationship had ended. When their younger son, John, graduated from grade school, Bev held a small party at the house. Since John wanted his father to come, Bev invited Jack. She was surprised at how well things went; Jack even stepped into the kitchen to talk with her while she was fixing some extra food. Some time afterward, when their older son,

Mark, asked that they sit together in the front pew at his wedding, they did not hesitate to agree.

We have seen that anger is a surface emotion. Because of its intensity, the first step is to deal with its symptoms—encourage people to exercise, hear them out as they vent their feelings. The main caution in finding outlets for expressing anger is not to intensify it by imagining an attack on its target, for example, the ex-partner.

Once they have calmed down, it is important to begin dealing with the underlying sources of their anger and discovering ways to resolve the problems that feed the anger. This helps move them past this "victim" stage.

Getting them to gradually forgive their ex-spouse, starting with small matters, is a major step toward getting them "unstuck." Meditation will help them acquire spiritual insight into their anger, achieve inner peace, see their problems in a broader perspective, and thus deal more effectively with them. Positive achievements will help them feel better about themselves and move on with their lives.

Sometimes, however, anger is more deeply rooted. Some long-standing difficulty that may have troubled them most of their life and contributed to their divorce may require further help. We will examine this "unfinished business" in the next chapter.

10

Unfinished Business

We view our lives through the lenses of our memories. If these memories are positive, we see ourselves as lovable, caring, strong, free and loving. If they are negative, we see ourselves as weak, unable to handle problems, insecure, unlovable and unloving.

Our past actions influence our future ones. To take a simple example, the birthday gift we bought last year will influence our choice of a gift next year. If the gift was well received, we have grounds for confidence in our taste and a motive to repeat the pleasure of giving. But if our gift was not well received, we may decide that we are unable to select a suitable gift for that person (and perhaps others as well) and may see the whole event as something to be avoided.

As individual experiences begin to form patterns in our minds, they increasingly influence our behavior, first as habits and then as character traits. Applying this to our example of gift-giving, a series of successful gifts could instill into a person the habit of giving generous gifts on many occasions beyond Christmas and birthdays, and to extend this giving beyond the circle of close family and friends. Eventually, this could instill deeper character traits of generosity and the enjoyment of others' company. A series of bad experiences with gift-giving could lead to further interpersonal problems, and eventually lead to deeper character traits of suspiciousness and isolation.

Family Structures

The most important source of our memories and experiences, especially when we are younger, is the family. Over a period of time, it evolves certain structures and patterns of interacting. Usually, the members take these structures and patterns for granted, but some rules may be more self-consciously acted out. For example, some families have a do-as-you-please policy, while others have a list of things that are not allowed. It is like belonging to a football team: You have to observe certain rules and regulations if you want to be a part of that team. Or, again, to play the trumpet in an orchestra, you have to play just at specified times, not whenever the mood strikes you.

Healthy families generally have four qualities: self-esteem, communication, rules and humor. Serious deficiencies in any of these areas can be carried on into the children's marriages. Hence, it is important to work on these areas in helping divorced people to heal their wounds and face the future. We will take up these qualities one by one.

Each member of a family needs a certain amount of self-esteem. A healthy self-esteem not only gives people the self-confidence to function well, but also helps them see value in others. People with low self-esteem do not function well, believe that life is not what it should be and criticize and blame others for whatever goes wrong. We have already talked about building up the divorced person's self-esteem; we would add here the importance of resolving any aspects of your own relationship with the divorced person that might adversely affect his or her self-esteem. You should not blame yourself, however, for the person's low self-esteem or assume the main responsibility for building it up; everyone must ultimately assume responsibility for his or her own attitudes and feelings. You can encourage them to work through this problem, though.

A second basic quality is good communication among the family members. You can observe this at family gatherings—does everyone join in and direct comments to each member in turn, or do some members seem to be excluded, ignored or even under attack? More deeply, does each one attempt to communicate and listen with care and love?

A graphic way of seeing this is through an exercise used in counselling families. The family members sit on the floor in a circle and one is handed a nerf ball. The counsellor observes what each does with it—hand, roll or toss it, playfully or angrily, to another; refuse to catch it; catch it and hold it or pass it on—and which members are included or overlooked in the game.

The third characteristic of a healthy family is rules. These include customs, stories and other traditions that have been handed down from one generation to the next and influence the members' behavior. These rules form a special bond between family members by giving them a common history and unique shared experiences, values and ways of acting. Rules also provide stability and a sense of rootedness.

Ideally, the rules will be flexible: adapted to changing circumstances and modified by the active participation of all the family members. Members know and accept the purpose of the rules and find them to be important ways of ordering and finding meaning in their lives.

Unfortunately, many family rules and customs are absorbed without thought, by a tacit acceptance that this is how things are or should be. Agnes, who had come with her husband for counselling, said she had to get home earlier than usual to prepare supper, adding that she had to cut the ends off the ham before baking it. When asked why she did that, she shrugged and said that this was the way her mother always did it. At the next session, she reported that her mother had been taught to do it by her own mother. When Agnes eventually asked her grandmother if she knew the purpose of this preparation, Grandma had explained that she had always cut the ham ends off because her pan was too small!

Although this custom, unquestioningly carried on, did little harm, many other customs and attitudes can prove harmful. Coming to understand their original purposes can be a liberating experience, and working out new rules in the light of experience and need is an important way of growing.

We have already talked about the fourth characteristic, humor, and the way it can relieve tensions and provide a more objective view of difficulties. What needs to be added in the context of the family is that there are special forms of humor in a family that can provide special ways for one member to help another deal with a problem such as divorce.

To put these four aspects in perspective: As the children in a healthy family grow, they acquire a sense of shared responsibility that includes distinctions between right and wrong. Rituals and traditions are an important bind among them. As all of the members interact, they create an overall balance that includes psychological, emotional, mental, physical and even spiritual significance.

Having this balance, the members can share in each other's joy and sadness while still respecting each other's privacy. The sharing can include coming together from great distances to observe holidays or helping a family member move. Helping each other through a period of sorrow, such as a death or a divorce, strengthens the bonds between them, helps them grow as individuals and modifies and deepens the family traditions.

Even more fundamental, but harder to define, are the relationships within the family. Ideally, all of the family members learn how to relate intimately to each other, to support each other, contribute to the common good, and develop a sense of simultaneously functioning as both a unique individual and part of a social unit. In short, they must learn to accept themselves and others, and to relate to other people.

Along with the structures, the family is a natural place for growth and healing. One of the subsystems that builds up in a family is the relationship between the mother and the father. A boundary around them gives them an area in which they can satisfy their own psychological needs and in which no intrusions by in-laws, children or anyone else are allowed.

This boundary system has certain requirements. Certain things are allowed between the two of them, giving them a safe space. However, this boundary should not exclude all others all the time; there has to be enough flexibility that they can bring in from their respective families and friends ''extra-family transactions.''

There also has to be flexibility within the relationship, so that each is free to exercise creativity and share things that are personally important. If the relationship is so fixed or rigid as to exclude such matters, it becomes impoverished.

The first concentric circle around this central relationship is the children. The children should not intrude into the central relationship, but the parents have obligations reaching out to the children. There are many kinds of relationships between parents and children, and these relationships have to change over time.

The third concentric circle includes other relatives and friends and the couple's social milieu, including their church, clubs and activities. The core relationship is always primary; putting other relationships between the two partners eventually causes a marriage to head into difficulty or even divorce.

In a healthy marriage, problems can be solved within the core relationship. Even a problem centered on the relationship itself, while it may cause turmoil, will move them into a new, higher level of complexity as they work through it, so that their relationship is enriched and strengthened. They learn intimacy, and how to relate to others with honesty, care and an openness to growth.

Perpetuation

When a couple divorces, they are confronted with a crisis and lose this central place for resolving it. They commonly lose confidence in their ability to achieve intimacy and fear trying lest they be hurt again. Moreover specific patterns of acting and feeling that may be present in one or both of the partners can further complicate the process.

The way we handle anger is closely tied in to our family system. For example, some families never talk about problems; others yell a lot. Think about how your family dealt with problems, and see to what degree you do these same things.

Specific experiences can have broader ramifications as they become patterns. Parents who have repeatedly lost their tempers with their children or failed to carry out their responsibilities as they see them may conclude that they are inadequate or morally reprehensible. This lack of confidence and self-esteem, in turn, could cause them to continue to relate poorly to their children and may also spill over into other areas, leading to other emotional problems, sexual dysfunction and other difficulties.

An isolated memory is usually not as powerful as a pattern of repeated memories; a pattern involved with an unresolved relational problem is the most powerful of all. For example, those who have unresolved conflicts with their parents or previous spouses are likely to find themselves enmeshed in similar conflicts in their present relationships. This, especially, is what this chapter refers to as "unfinished business."

In an extreme example of unfinished business, Sarah had never gotten along well with her daughter Becky, and she became extremely angry when Becky divorced her husband. Becky, in turn, had never found much satisfaction with either her mother or her children, and so did not want custody of the children. Thus, when her ex-husband moved to another city with the children, neither Sarah nor Becky had much contact with them. Sarah loved her grandchildren, but had little prospect of having much contact with them until she could resolve her differences with Becky.

Habits and the deeper character traits that correspond to them are influenced by earlier experiences, and are continually reinforced by the memories of those experiences; to complete the circle, new experiences that follow the same pattern create new memories that reinforce it further. Such a self-defeating circle commonly develops during a divorce.

Jack and Bev's divorce came as a shock to their parents. The couple had moved out of town shortly after their marriage, so they saw their parents primarily on major holidays and occasional vacation visits. On these occasions, the parents had seen their growing family and apparent happiness—much in keeping with the smiling pictures they periodically received and dutifully pasted into their family album.

The divorce brought the parents into the conflict in two ways. First, Jack and Bev frequently tried to enlist their parents' support in their extended dispute over the financial settlements. Second, the divorce caused each of them to renew old conflicts with their parents.

Jack faced his parents' general disapproval of divorce and their disappointment in him. They did not say much, for their habit was to grieve in private; this habit, in turn, made something as public as a divorce trouble them all the more. Jack's immediate reaction to their disapproval was to blame them, especially his father, for emphasizing rules and work rather than intimacy. He said they had never taught him how to be close to another person. His parents also found themselves renewing old fights with each other—about the importance of work versus their relationship, about the need to uphold standards with their children versus the importance of being supportive, and so on.

Such opening of old wounds and increased blaming intensified both Jack's and his parents' pain. Initially, the intensified pain caused Jack and his parents to put some emotional distance between them, so they could allow their feelings to subside. They eventually sought counselling and were able to talk over some of their long-standing problems. Coming to a better understanding of their own relationship helped remove some of their sense of inadequacy, and this improvement, in turn, gave them some faith in their ability to resolve their own problems and establish emotional links with others.

As we saw earlier, Jack and Bev finally began meeting each other without their lawyers, and were able to work out both their financial differences and continuing shared responsibilities toward their children. A key element was their love for their children. The same love moved the grandparents to agree to join in the counselling and to back off from Jack and Bev's conflicts so that the divorcing couple could work things out.

Jack's family blamed Bev more than him for the divorce. Because the feelings ran high on both sides, they had virtually broken all contact with each other. However, Jack's parents strove to maintain some contact with their grandchildren by sending cards at every occasion— Christmas, Easter, birthdays, even Halloween. Despite her anger, Bev did not want to cut the children off from their grandparents, and so had them send cards and thank-you letters.

The exchange of cards and letters kept the relationship alive during these difficult times. After three years, the feelings on both sides had cooled down considerably. Jack's parents felt the time was opportune to invite Bev out to lunch. Everything went well and as a result the grandchildren were able to maintain an important kinship relationship.

In another case, Mark eventually came to understand how his unresolved conflicts with his parents undermined his marriage. When he was in high school, he had many fights with his parents. Sometimes he blew up, telling them that they did not know anything about life and that he was not about to let them tell him anything. More commonly, he retreated into silence. As a result he formed the habit of distancing himself from others and had two equally ineffective ways of dealing with conflict—fleeing from it rather than resolving it. These habits, and the self-image they created, helped to undermine his marriage.

This insight inspired Mark to talk over some of his long-standing differences with his parents. He found it hard to begin, because his history of personal conflicts seemed like an unrelieved record of pain and failure. Despite some bumpy going at the beginning, however, he and his parents were able to resolve some of their differences and, in the process, found love on both sides. Mark found that he was loved more than he had realized (and therefore was lovable), and found that he loved them (and therefore was capable of loving). With this new self-confidence and improved relationship skills, he was better prepared for forming future relationships.

Forgiveness

Juanita had trouble even talking about forgiveness, because she feared that full forgiveness would oblige her to take back her ex-husband. Her divorce group pointed out that forgiveness is not merely for the sake of some-one else, but is even more important for oneself. By hold-ing onto grievances, one gets stuck and cannot begin healing and moving on with life. Juanita agreed with this observation, but did not see how she could put it into practice, considering how strong her feelings were.

Greg responded that he, too, had felt it impossible to forgive his ex-wife for all the pain he had gone through. What had helped him break out of this impasse was the idea of a step-by-step forgiveness, starting with minor areas. Juanita found this useful also. She began by reflecting that her ex-husband had not had much educa-tion about relationships. This realization enabled her to forgive him for some relatively small acts of neglect and inconsiderateness.

Keep in mind in dealing with forgiveness and other unfinished business that the move from accepting an ab-stract principle to putting it into practice can take a long time. People may hear an idea several times before it ac-tually clicks and they see how it can work in their own lives.

Guilt

Many divorced people struggle with expectations typically formed and sustained by their family, church and society. You can help them to accept themselves bet-ter by helping to provide a loving environment. Also, helping them lower their expectations of themselves will help to relieve the heavy burden of guilt they may feel. All of us make mistakes; unrealistically high expectations doom us to a vicious circle of frustration and guilt.

Although people often feel that their religious beliefs encourage guilt, excessive guilt can actually undermine a person's religion. Facing what seem to be impossible demands, a person may reject the God behind such demands as cold, distant and uncaring. At the other extreme, those who continually fall short of their ideals may conclude that they have cut themselves off from God's love. Such dark thoughts can dim a person's perception of God's love. Those who suffer from this kind of pain need to treat themselves gently. Treating them gently yourself will help as well.

It is important for troubled people to believe that God always offers love and forgiveness freely and unconditionally. The door to God's love is always unlocked; it is up to us to open it. However, God also gave us freedom to take or leave his gifts. We tend to keep asking God to forgive a particular wrong that we're suffering from; however, when God forgives something, he also forgets about it. When we bring the matter up again, his response is, ''What?''

Changing the Family System

In a similar way, it is important for troubled persons to know that the door to their families is unlocked, that they can always return and find acceptance. The family may very well find itself challenged to provide this acceptance, but it will grow through confronting that challenge.

The family system changes whenever one of its members changes, because the others have to begin to relate to that member differently. The entire family has to focus on its structures, values and customs. In showing love and support for a divorced member of your family, you may be challenging your own long-held beliefs and those of others in the family. Done in the proper spirit, this can lead to growth in understanding and deeper love among your family members.

"Home"

When we were young, our parents or some loving adult brought us into a home. "Home" gradually took on deep emotional meanings, based upon the love we felt from our family and that we showed toward them. It is not so much a place as it is relationships. Seeing one's family home years later, now owned by strangers, may evoke memories of the past but the house itself will no longer feel like home. On the other hand, those memories of family and home continue to be a powerful influence in one's life, even when one is thousands of miles from the house and not even thinking of it.

We can now help the divorced find a "home" or rebuild their lost home. In the gospels, we find that Jesus constantly used the image of inviting everyone to a banquet. In Luke 14:15-24 he tells of a lord who invited many different people, including strangers, to the banquet table. While many turned down the invitation, the lord continued reaching out. We too can continue offering a stable loving relationship to the divorced, even when they initially reject our overtures. Even if they do not seem to appreciate our offer, knowing that they have a "home" to turn to is meaningful to them.

Leaving Home

Home should also provide a point of reference. Whether this is helpful depends to a considerable extent upon the way we leave it to venture forth in the world. There are three basic ways of leaving home. In the first, one leaves with bitter arguing and resentment, like a gunfighter backing out of the door of a saloon, intent upon shooting at the building. One doesn't pay much heed to where one is headed, because all attention is directed back at the house. Such preoccupation makes new relationships difficult.

The second way is to decide that those at home are ignorant of modern times, turn one's back to the house, and run anywhere, so long as it is away from home. Although one's back is turned to the home, one's energy is directed to running away from it, leaving little energy for new people and relationships.

The third method of leaving is to reach out for complete self-fulfillment, cherishing the love that's still at home. It's like going out the door sideways; in this way, walking down the street, one can look to the right or left to see where one is going, yet easily see the home. This stable reference point gives a better sense of direction, gives a sense of being lovable and loving, and offers a secure refuge that in turn leads to more willingness to be venturesome.

How a person leaves home, whether that of the parents or a previous marriage, profoundly affects the next home, especially when there is unfinished business. People who leave home in a hostile manner and engage in a similar conflict with their spouse tend to leave their marriage. Somehow, the two conflicts become entwined, with the same result. Only resolution of their original conflict would enable them to overcome their second conflict. This seems to hold true in a majority of the cases.

Normally, the healing cannot take place for some time, perhaps as long as three years. This can be a long, painful period for the parents of the divorced. The positive side of it is that parents can play a key role in the healing process. In helping to resolve long-standing problems, they can play a key role in their children's future relationships. They can also play a key role in helping their grandchildren through the trying time of the divorce, as we shall see in the next chapter.

11

Children

As children grow up in a family, some seem to go along easily, while others seem to bump into every door or situation. But even the children who seem to take things easily experience tension in coping with more demanding challenges at home, in school and among friends. When confronted with divorce, an adult solution to an adult problem, their tension multiplies. In order to help a child whose parents are divorced, it is important to understand these events as a child does.

To children, the family seems a ''given'': Mom, Dad, the house, brothers and sisters, pets and all other parts of their world appear as permanent as the sky and the grass. Then, one day, Mom or Dad is gone. They may have to move into a strange, perhaps markedly less pleasant, home. Like people who have experienced an earthquake, children whose stable world tumbled down without warning may henceforth look with distrust upon even the firmest ground.

Brent, aged seven, related that one day Dad simply moved away. This caused Brent to worry that some day in the future he might wake up and find that Mom had disappeared, too. This fear of abandonment is common, especially in younger, more dependent, children. Preschool children may exhibit regression, such as abandoning their toilet training, or they may have trouble sleeping, be habitually sad or irritable or show increased aggression.

After Brent had verbalized his fears, he began, with help and encouragment, to list the people who would take care of him if something were to happen to his mom. He eventually had a list of six people, including his Dad, his grandparents and some aunts and uncles. This helped lessen his fears of abandonment.

In talking things over with children, especially younger ones, it is important to let them set the pace and not overwhelm them with more than they can take in. Sam observed that his son, Charlie, who was five, could handle only a small amount of information at a time. Sam had to rein himself in: He was anxious to explain the entire matter of the divorce right away but had to give Charlie only a bit at a time. In fact, Charlie often repeated a question that had been answered earlier, apparently as a way of dealing gingerly with one small part of the hurt at a time.

Cody, on the other hand, wished his parents would ask him whether he wanted to know anything about the divorce, but he was stymied because his parents did not volunteer any information and he was too shy to ask. He also worried that his father did not love him since he never called. Cody was part of a group of small children whose parents were divorced. When he related his predicament during a meeting, the other children joined in with their own stories of difficulties in meeting with the non-custodial parent, especially for a short, unscheduled visit when they wanted to talk over something. The group felt that someone neutral, like a counsellor, could best step in here. A friend or relative who has friendly relations with both parents could also step in effectively.

When asked how things could be made easier for them, one of the chief concerns the group expressed was that their parents listen to them when there was a time conflict with their scheduled visitation—for example, when school activities occurred at the same time. One of the group hit upon flexibility as the quality they needed from their parents to resolve such conflicts.

Linda said she was never allowed to visit her paternal grandparents because her mother was fighting with that side of the family. The others in the group agreed that it was important to see both sets of grandparents, aunts, uncles and cousins (and nice to receive presents from both sides of the family, too). The group also concluded that both Linda and her grandparents had the right to see each other. In fact, a growing number of states are making this right of visitation by grandparents explicit in their laws. In counselling, this right is seen as an important part of each person's heritage; through the development of the "kinship bond" each person learns the factors that have and will continue to influence his or her development. Much of this heritage is passed down through the family stories and traditions. Grandparents are important here, especially after a divorce. Without this connection to the absent parent's side of the family, the children lose at least half of their heritage.

Maggie, Randy and Jo felt uneasy whenever their parents talked about money and support. Such talk stimulated the children's fears that they might all starve to death. Dusty related how he had suffered from the same fear until one of his aunts had helped him get up his courage to talk this over with his parents. This had taken place about six months earlier; now that his parents seldom mention these concerns in front of him, he has felt much more secure.

Jack and Bev's children exemplify some typical reactions. The ways in which others helped them offer valuable models for dealing with adolescent children of a divorced couple.

At first, 13-year-old John, the youngest, imagined that he had caused the divorce. Like most parents, Jack and Bev did not fight about deeply personal matters in front of their children; typically, most of the arguments that the children witnessed were centered on themselves, such as disagreements about what the children should be required to do, how they should be punished and what the parents should or shouldn't be expected to do for them. Thus, it was easy for a younger child like John to see fights as a cause of the divorce and himself as the cause of the fights.

Younger children, especially, believe in "magic," that is, the power to control others' thoughts, actions and even fate. This is not the same thing as the delightful or scary powers ascribed to fairy-tale characters; even very young children know that these are make-believe. On the other hand, even many adults unwittingly believe that one person can change another with almost casual effort. History books, fiction and television shows depict the influence of individuals—how one person changes many other lives, even saves an entire nation from disaster. Many dramas show a character uttering a single sentence that either pushes another person into despair or an evil course of action or saves the person from a life of crime.

Influenced by such pervasive views, children who have wished some evil onto another have often felt guilty later when the evil actually occurred. Often, too, they easily misinterpret what they see or are told. It is not uncommon, for example, for children to express their discomfort at seeing their parents quarrel, and for the parents, feeling defensive, to retort that, since many fights were occasioned by the children, better behavior by them would greatly reduce their parents' fights. If, subsequently, the parents announce their separation without previous warning, it may seem like black magic to their children, who may then see their misbehavior as its source.

This sort of reasoning led John to conclude that he had caused Jack and Bev's divorce. Guilt and a strong desire to re-establish their more stable home motivated him to seek to bring his parents back together again. After all, if his magic had torn them apart, could it not bring them back together again?

When Bev's parents became aware of John's matchmaking efforts, they casually asked him about it one day. John told them of his hopes and gradually revealed his feelings of guilt. They then talked to Bev about this. Fortunately, this occurred when she and Jack had begun cooperating with regard to the children, so they sat down with John and explained that he was not to blame, that big people have their own differences. Of course, other significant people can explain such things to the children, but if the parents can be enlisted, this is the best way.

Another reason why children this age especially work on reconciling their parents is the pressure of divided loyalties. This inherent byproduct of divorce is intensified when the parents fight over their children's allegiance—for example, when one parent tries to prevent the other from seeing the children, demands that the children blame the other for the divorce, uses the children as messengers to the other parent, or, worse yet, asks the children to spy while they are visiting. Larry, who was 15, told his grandparents that he loved both of his parents but was tired of them playing games with him caught in the middle. The grandparents then talked their son into meeting with his ex-wife at a neutral site every four months to sort out their differences, at least those centered on Larry. As his parents settled their differences, Larry found it easier to get along with both of them, and he fared better at school as well.

Some children may seek a friend or relative with whom they can discuss the problem; others may try to deny that the divorce is permanent, so that getting them to talk about it is like peeling away the layers from an onion. Like younger children, they may show uncharacteristic anger in their everyday actions and may experience sleep problems. They may also cause trouble at school in an attempt to force their parents back together.

A combination of desperation and immaturity may goad young adolescents into taking rash action. Two 13-year-olds, Robin and Debbie, had held furtive conferences that aroused their parents' suspicions; Robin's mother and Debbie's father acted by sending the girls for counselling.

Between many nervous laughs, poppings of bubble gum, and sidelong glances at each other, the girls complained that no one understood them so they were planning to run away together and get an apartment of their own. They would spend their mornings listening to music and their afternoons looking at the boys at the roller-skating rink; school did not figure into their plans.

After pouring out their complaints for the better part of two sessions, they listed their needs on a blackboard. When asked how they thought that the divorce was affecting their parents, the girls eventually concluded that their parents were having a rough time, too, and made a list of their parents' needs that probably were not being met. Accordingly, they decided to talk things over with their parents instead of running away. Just having someone listen seriously to their problems had made them feel much better, so that they were able to start seeing some things from others' points of view as well.

One thing that helped John was Jack's renting an apartment within walking distance of the house. This enabled John and the other children to visit when they wanted. This freedom to see both parents helped limit the struggle with divided loyalties.

The visits were especially important to John, for they kept his relationship with his father tangible. Younger children who have never seen the departed parent's new home worry how that parent will get along without a refrigerator, a bed and other necessities. Simply seeing such things is reassuring. As a concerned friend or relative, then, you can encourage the parents to see to it that their children maintain contact, perhaps offer to bring the children for a visit, or, if visits are not feasible, you might try bringing pictures of the absent parent's home.

Adolescent children, being more involved with friends and outside activities, and immersing themselves in the transition from the home to the world outside, generally feel less threatened by instability at home than their younger siblings, though they are, of course, affected by it. They are disturbed by open conflicts between their parents because this focuses attention on the home situation; when things go more smoothly, the adolescents are able to focus outward and so can distance themselves from the divorce. What tends to bother them more is their parents' perceived moral shortcomings.

Jack and Bev's 16-year-old daughter, Terri, saw her parents' divorce as a serious breach of the rules that they had inculcated in her and the other children. Psychologically, she felt the need for a stable set of rules against which to define herself, even if that meant at least partly rebelling against them in order to work out a stable version of her own. Of course, rules are not truly stable if no one keeps them, and the parents' stability in their relationship is a promise that she, too, would be able to establish permanent relationships.

As in the case of John, Jack and Bev sat down with Terri and reassured her of their continuing love and care for her, even though the two of them could no longer live

together. Although this did not entirely remove her concerns, Terri was reassured by the stability of their relationship toward her.

Another girl of Terri's age, Molly, experienced a
much greater shock. With tears in her eyes, she said her
mom had always inculcated in her and her sister the
rules they were supposed to live by. However, now her
mom was divorcing and had begun running around with
some other fellow—some of Molly's friends had seen
them out after four in the morning. Molly showed a mix-
ture of disbelief and anger.

After she had expressed her pain and had somewhat calmed down, she began exploring the matter. She
came to realize from stories and examples that people do
not always live up to all that they believe in. This did not
mean, however, that they did not really believe in those
ideals. It merely meant that, being human, they sometimes fell short. The important thing was to keep on
striving, even if it took years. Molly admitted that she,
too, had failings, and had found encouragement when
her parents showed her love at such times. She finally
concluded that although she did not approve of her
mom's behavior she still loved her.

As the oldest of Jack and Bev's children, 22-year-old
Art felt called upon to take over for his absent father. Accordingly, he announced his intention of staying home
to take care of Bev and the younger children. This time,
Jack and Bev took the initiative and sat down with Art,
explaining to him that this was not his role. Again,
though this is best done by the parents, other close relatives can help an older child understand this.

A further complication in dealing with children
arises because the divorced person is a son or daughter
as well as a parent. Roles need to be clarified and responsibilities established in the confusion that often accompa-
nies a divorce.

A parent's role must change as a child grows up. A parent sets down rules and regulations, tells the off-spring what to do, emphasizes "shoulds." This role essentially ends when the child reaches 18 years of age. The father or mother role is that of offering love and support, of modeling giving, receiving and loving. It involves a role of forgiveness that never ends.

If the "parent" role continues too long, it gets in the way of intimacy and may undermine the child's self-confidence. When a person is struggling through a divorce, it is easy for his or her own parents to fall back into their "parenting" role, especially if their son or daughter moves back home with the grandchildren. In trying to "fix" the pain, the parents do not allow the person to grow through the hurt. This can create the common problem of tri-generational enmeshment. The divorced parent can feel confused about acting both as a young child and as a parent, and the grandchildren can become confused about who their real parent is.

Bev encountered this problem with her parents. They had always been supportive of her and, following her break with Jack, she and the children stayed with them. They began treating her as a hurt child, however, and also began taking charge of the grandchildren. Bev needed to stand on her own feet, not be treated as a child, and her children grew increasingly confused about who was in charge. After a few months, Bev decided to move out and set up her own home again.

Nine-year-old Megan was having similar difficulties. After the divorce, she was placed in the custody of her father, George. When they first moved into his parents' home, Megan enjoyed having her grandparents around. She soon found everyone giving her orders—often conflicting ones. Things became especially confusing when the grandparents disagreed with George and started telling him how to parent.

They needed to have tri-generational enmeshment explained to them. It was pointed out that the grandparents were still parenting George as well as taking charge of Megan. In effect, they were making both George and Megan children, which confused George's role as parent. It was important that George be the parent; he and his parents had to work out their differences when Megan was not present. Later on, Megan reported that things were going much better at home.

Two other difficulties frequently arise among the adults: The parents often differ in their parenting styles, and the grandparents may end up blaming themselves for their children's divorce.

For some time, Connie had been upset that when her four-year-old, P.J., visited his father, many of the rules and rituals she worked so hard to inculcate were totally ignored, which meant she had to start all over again upon P.J.'s return. After several counselling sessions, she came to see that P.J. did fine with his father, and that this continued relationship was most important to him. She also conceded that since she and her ex-husband had often disagreed on many other matters, it stood to reason that they would disagree on parenting, too. The father's different approach did not mean that he did not love P.J., just that he had different ways of expressing his love.

In another case, Dottie and Bernard expressed their sorrow over their daughter's divorce. Besides feeling concern for her, they felt that her divorce showed that they had failed as parents. It helped to assure them that feeling sad over the divorce was normal, but that it was important for them to avoid getting caught in the brokenness of the divorce. They had done their best as parents at the time, so they should not second-guess themselves now with the wisdom of hindsight. That is like imaging what a killing one could have made on the stock market if one had known ten years ago what one knows now. Their daughter was now 32 and needed to take responsibility for her own behavior. In accepting this view of things, Dottie and Bernard felt better and were able to be more truly helpful. Their new attitude also helped their daughter take firmer control of her own life, instead of blaming others and feeling sorry for herself.

It is important for friends and relatives to avoid inter-family fights, to listen to the children and to help them maintain ties with both sides of the family. It is important to make sure that younger children know that the divorce does not mean that they will not be taken care of, and that they are not to blame for the divorce. They need not be protected from the truth about the divorce, though it is important to give them only as much information as they can handle.

The children should not be made pawns or messengers in their parents' fights. They need not be ''bought'' with expensive gifts. What they need above all is for the adults in their lives to continue acting as adults—parents, aunts, uncles, grandparents—and not as ''pals'' to the children. Children need the stability of clearly defined roles at this point in their lives.

Adolescent children often change their attitudes toward their parents after a divorce, and they may express great anger about it. For some, the divorce will be only a temporary interference with their growing up; however, those who were having trouble growing up before the divorce may experience serious troubles after it. The ones who fare best are those who distance themselves from the divorce. Like the divorcing parent, kids working on many other scenes in their tapestry will be less affected by the damages to their family scenes than those whose tapestry is almost exclusively devoted to their home life.

12

Storytelling

Telling people what to do about difficult, emotion-laden situations is usually not effective. Unless they are seeking answers, advice at best will be ignored and at worst will incite their defensiveness, which will move them to rationalize, and thereby reinforce, their present attitudes.

In most cases, people fail to take obviously needed action, like finding a job or losing dangerously excessive weight, not because they don't know what they should do, but because strong emotions block them from accepting and acting upon their knowledge. Even when there are no strong opposing emotions, abstract ideas rarely move someone to concrete actions. Even St. Paul tells us that good intentions frequently fall short: ''In my inmost self I dearly love God's law, but I see that acting on my body there is a different law which battles against the law in my mind'' (Rom 7:22-23).

On occasion, a person may need, and ask for, direct advice. A genuine request—not one merely seeking support for a decision already made or arguments to confute and thereby prove the hopelessness of any action—signifies that the divorced person wants to act and so will be able to profit from advice. Even if your advice is not followed, it may help the person define what needs to be done. Your experience with a person's reactions to advice will soon show you whether or not the requests for advice are genuine.

Even when the request for direct advice is genuine, it may be wise to give it by indirection—for example, by telling a story about someone else. Consider what may appear as a minor difference in the approaches to the following situation. A divorced mother was becoming frantic over her child's defiant behavior at home and at school. Her parents lived far away, and she and her ex-husband had not spoken since the divorce.

Direct advice might be, "Come to terms with your feelings about the divorce, then discuss the problem with your ex-husband. Only when both of you accept the divorce and become involved with your son will you be able to help him deal with it and feel accepted."

The storytelling approach would relate how you, someone you know or someone you read about dealt with a similar situation in this way, and how this helped the child. Such a story conveys essentially the same suggestion. The difference is that advice "tells" people what to do, and forces them to accept or reject your counsel, whereas a story about how someone else dealt with a similar situation turns the immediate attention away from the divorced person. It is always easier to talk about others' touchy problems than your own. Even this little distancing can make the listener less defensive.

An important implication in telling a story is that it simply represents information; the listener is free to draw his or her own conclusions. Your attitude is crucial here in leaving the implications open-ended.

Remember, too, that while a story does not press for immediate acceptance or rejection, nevertheless, because it relates closely to the divorced person's own situation, it can stir up defensiveness. He or she might say, "That's easy for that person, but my situation is more complicated, and I'm not capable of doing things like that."

The divorced have the resources—the tapestry threads—to rebuild their lives. Insights into people's inner strengths have caused us to stress encouragement as the single most important help that you can give a divorced friend or relative. Storytelling is a special form of encouragement; it expresses confidence in people's ability to come to their own conclusions. It can also bypass rational arguments, which usually leave another person unmoved, and appeal directly to their feelings. Such an approach offers them the reassurance and motivation they need to move ahead.

Changing emotions is a difficult and gradual process. The type of story that is helpful here is only obliquely related to the divorcing person's situation. General stories of people coping with problems unrelated to divorce or of people setting and realizing goals can leave a general impression that it is possible for people to act upon and achieve goals they set for themselves. One or two such stories may not accomplish much, and over-obvious attempts to cheer the divorced may backfire, but the judicious use of many stories over time will eventually have an effect.

Fairy tales can serve as a good source of stories, since they are significantly removed from the person's direct circumstances and yet deal with the broad aspects of human experience. Since they are well known, they can serve as brief examples, without detailed retelling. You can also freely reinterpret the tales, not merely retell them. For example, you may hint that waiting for a fairy godmother to improve one's state is unrealistic, even if it worked for Cinderella. Beauty and the Beast may suggest that love and patience bring deep rewards, that sharing suffering can lead to genuine happiness.

In using this method of storytelling, remember the following points: Be positive; introduce the stories as interesting anecdotes; try to be spontaneous, as though the story is a natural comment on the conversation taking place. Finally, be patient—this is a long-term method, not a quick fix.

Below is an imaginative retelling of the story of the woman at the well. It tells a story of a woman five times divorced who found healing and salvation through the compassion and acceptance of Jesus. Consider how the story applies most of the principles we've discussed in the book.

The Woman at the Well

The sun glared down and she could neither rest nor think of work. Dishes and breakfast scraps still on the table attracted little attention in the unkempt house. Who cared? Certainly not that lazy lout snoring in the corner. Nor did she have to worry about visitors.

She had made a few fitful tugs at her tapestry, only to tear out the scene she had been struggling with off and on for the past two months. She couldn't get it right, and it was looking more ragged all the time. She should probably just chuck it.

All she felt at this moment was a tug-of-war between her parched throat and the lassitude that made her dread trudging through the heat and dust all the way to Jacob's Well.

Finally, thirst won out and she heaved herself to her feet. There was one consoling thought: The punishing heat would long ago have driven her neighbors indoors. She could lug the water home without encountering those busybodies and their smug looks and whisperings. You'd think they'd have tired of it by now. They themselves were hardly model wives and mothers, but at least *they* hadn't been handed on from one man to another!

Let them have their husbands! Let them preen themselves over their imagined superiority. What did she care?

As she dragged through the dusty streets, bent under her jar, she wondered what genius had built the city down in this sweltering valley. The men could explain the military advantages of commanding the crossroads from the Jordan, the coast, Galilee, and Jerusalem. Well, those crossroads had brought the Romans right to their gates, so now the city didn't have to worry about any other invaders. With a bitter smile, she conceded that the military design was fitting after all, for life itself was surely a ceaseless battle.

Her toughness helped her find a way to avoid her enemies, but she sometimes felt it would be a relief to have someone to talk to, if only to break up the monotony of the journey to the well. Everything was so sunbleached that her eyes ached from the blankness before her—blank houses in the blank dust under the colorless sky. A couple of mangy dogs growled half-heartedly and then slumped back down in the shade.

As she neared the well, she was startled to see someone resting there. Just what she needed! At least it was a man, so she wouldn't have to speak to him. Coming up to the edge of the well, she noted that he was a stranger, probably a Jew traveling to or from Jerusalem—someone else to look down upon her for being a "half-breed" Samaritan who worshipped in the wrong temple. It was almost enough to make her laugh. With all her troubles, did she need to journey all the way to the Jerusalem Temple just to say, "Thanks for nothing"?

Her best strategy here was to get her water in a no-nonsense way and head straight back. A little rest after a drink and a splash of the cool water might have given her a little more energy for the return trip but, no matter, she could lie about the rest of the day at home.

It took time to fasten the rope to her empty jar and lower it into the well, and forever to haul the filled jar back up. Finally, panting and sweating, she set the jar on the ground and began tugging at the knot.

''Give me a drink.''

The man's voice startled her. Her first impulse was to grab her jar and walk away, but then indignation pushed aside her fear. So, Samaritans weren't good enough to worship or socialize with, but they were good enough to wait on the Jews!

Scowling at the traveler, she demanded, ''What? You are a Jew, and you ask me, a Samaritan, for a drink?''

The stranger's response took her aback: ''If you only knew what God is offering and who it is that is asking you for a drink, you would have been the one to ask, and he would have given you living water.''

She was dealing with a loony! With exaggerated motions, she glanced at the depths of the well and then at his empty hands. ''You have no bucket, sir, and the well is deep: how could you get this living water? Are you a greater man than our father Jacob who gave us this well and drank from it himself with his sons and his cattle?''

Her mind was awakening to the combat now. For the moment, she was no longer the outcast of the city, but at one with its other inhabitants, defending their status as equal children of Jacob.

The stranger ignored the polemics, pursuing instead his own line of thought. ''Whoever drinks this water will get thirsty again; but anyone who drinks the water that I shall give will never be thirsty again: the water that I shall give will turn into a spring inside him, welling up to eternal life.''

Better and better! She began to feel a bit amused at this crack-brain, and decided to test how far he would go. ''Sir,'' she said with exaggerated politeness, ''give me some of that water, so that I may never get thirsty and never have to come here again to draw water.''

The stranger again threw her off the track: "Go and call your husband, and come back here."

Her cheeks flushed, but, with an effort, she choked off the tremor in her voice and affected a matter-of-fact tone: "I have no husband."

The stranger looked deeply into her eyes, as if he could see right inside her. His answer startled her: "You are right to say, 'I have no husband'; for although you have had five, the one you have now is not your husband. You spoke the truth there."

Though her face was already flushed from the heat, she could feel a hot wave of blood swirl through her head. Even before this outsider she had to feel ashamed! How could he have heard about her? He had obviously just arrived, and no other inhabitant was in sight. As she valiantly forced herself to meet his gaze, she felt a deep, quiet source of strength in him. Ah! There was a tack to turn the subject from her private life.

"I see you are a prophet, sir." Now to get back to the Jewish-Samaritan controversy, where she could lash back as the defender of the city. "Our fathers worshipped on this mountain, while you say that Jerusalem is the place where one ought to worship." She looked at him expectantly, ready to become lost in a good argument.

Once again, the stranger refused to become sidetracked in legalistic arguments. "Believe me, woman, the hour is coming when you will worship the Father neither on this mountain nor in Jerusalem. You worship what you do not know; for salvation comes from the Jews. But the hour will come—in fact is here already—when true worshippers will worship the Father in spirit and in truth: that is the kind of worshipper the Father wants. God is spirit, and those who worship must worship in spirit and truth."

As he spoke, she found her defensiveness and combativeness being replaced with simultaneous feelings of peace and hopeful excitement. This man spoke with quiet authority. And though he seemed to know all about her, he accepted her and spoke of a new, higher form of worship that pushed aside the old barriers of race, sects and legalisms that had always shut her out. Instead of worrying about her ancestors, place of worship, or past errors, he urged her to find a special relationship with God as a father, and to worship in spirit and truth.

Her sense of liberation and of sudden hope for a deeper, more meaningful religion that would quicken her life brought to mind the ancient promise from God. Looking at him closely now, with her heart beating faster and her breath held expectantly, she broached the subject: "I know that the Messiah is coming; and when he comes he will tell us everything."

The stranger turned his penetrating look fully upon her and said quietly, "I who am speaking to you am he."

Everything fell into place. She couldn't give any theological justifications for her belief, but every part of her being cried, "Yes!"

She noticed a group of men, also Jews who had been traveling, come up to them. They looked puzzled—certainly, she reflected, it was unusual for a Jew to talk with any woman by herself, much less a Samaritan—but they didn't say anything. This stranger was obviously their leader, and one did not question such deep authority.

Suddenly, her sense of elation found her brimming with energy. She had to share this good news with her neighbors! She placed her water jar before the stranger, gestured that all should help themselves, then hurried back toward the city.

As she half walked, half ran, her feet seemed to spring off the ground. The sun filled her with energy, and she marveled at how the white houses gleamed under the deep blue of the sky, setting off the deep green of scattered date palms.

She was amazed how quickly she made it back to her neighborhood. She saw several women talking together inside a doorway; instead of rushing out of earshot, she eagerly ran up to them with her news.

As she drew near, she heard remarks about some strangers seeking food. Then abrupt silence gripped the group as they stared at her, perplexed both by her joining them and by her joyousness.

''Come and see a man who has told me everything I ever did; I wonder if he is the Christ?'' It didn't take much persuasion to gather a crowd. Her claims increased the others' curiosity about this prophet and his followers, and offered an excuse to investigate.

As she led the crowd back to the well, her confidence swelled. She called out to every curious person who appeared in a window or doorway, and boldly went up to groups of men—both those that she hardly knew and those that she knew only too well.

While the people listened to the stranger's teachings, she felt her horizons expanding: Her own mind was opening, and she felt pride in having led her people to this prophet. She never wanted this moment to end. Couldn't Jesus stay? Yes, others took up the call, they'd gladly put him and his disciples up.

And so, for two more days, Jesus stayed and taught them. The first night, she found the energy to bathe and wash clothes so that she and her man could appear with proper respect. She even reached into her memory for the recipes to cook some special dishes to contribute to the ''potluck'' meals the village shared with Jesus and his followers. A couple of the neighboring women complimented her on her cooking. More importantly, she enjoyed it herself—she'd begun to think that she had lost either her skills or her taste for food.

All too soon, Jesus moved on to Galilee. But he left behind a group of people devoted to him and his new teachings. She had a place now. The law of love was stronger than any past failings. Someone cared, and she had made an important contribution to the community—hadn't she discovered the long-awaited Messiah and brought the others to him?

Of course, some had to remonstrate with her over her pride. They informed her, ''Now we no longer believe because of what you told us; we have heard ourselves and we know that he really is the savior of the world.''

Well, she laughed to herself, maybe she did act too self-important at times. She could stand—even profit from—a little healthy criticism now and then. Whatever her faults, she still felt good about having made a lasting contribution to the community and playing a continuing role as the best-informed witness of Jesus' ministry to them.

After setting her house in order for the day, she eagerly sat down at her tapestry, so bursting with exciting new scenes to weave that her fingers could not keep up with her thoughts and feelings.

13

Action Checklist

This chapter briefly describes the most common problems that you are likely to encounter when helping your divorced relative or friend. After each problem, we summarize our recommended course of action. These summaries are necessarily incomplete and oversimplified; they are intended to jog your memory of reading the book, not to stand by themselves.

Attitude: The way you think about divorced people will eventually speak louder than anything you do. If you see them as capable people who will eventually overcome their present difficulties and rebuild their lives, you have a reliable guide to helping them, and your attitude will subtly bolster their self-confidence.

Realize that most divorces happen because the partners gradually break off communication with each other, not because of major faults or injuries. Even if some divorced people seem culpable, it is helpful to reflect how all of us, including the greatest leaders and saints in history, have had weaknesses but have been able to accompish a great deal in spite of them. It helps to meditate upon the loving way that Jesus dealt with sinners.

Encouragement: The divorced have lost the person nearest them, and probably a number of in-laws and friends as well; they face additional everyday tasks that their spouse used to handle; they typically have less money to work with; they may have to undertake major tasks such as housekeeping or finding an outside job for which they have little experience or training. A great deal of self-confidence is needed to undertake so many difficult tasks at the same time.

Your attitude is the single most important way of giving encouragement. If your actions show that you are sincere, words of encouragement will help, too.

At first, they may need to be by themselves a good deal of the time, to let their wounds heal and to protect themselves from new injuries. After a few months, however, they should not continue focusing inward on their injuries. Gently lead them into new activities with new people, such as a church group or a club. If they shun company, show them that you are standing by them by sending a card or calling up now and then.

Overload: They will often feel overwhelmed by their new responsibilities and the lack of a partner to pitch in. Staying calm and listening to their story will help them sort things out and calm them down as well. Some practical help, like baby-sitting or helping them with an unfamiliar task, will give them a chance to regain their equanimity. Gently suggest that they gain a little control over their lives by doing some little things they haven't done before, like opening a checking account or cooking a simple breakfast, and then give them a pat on the back for their achievement.

Anger: This can be expressed in many other, subtler ways than violence and yelling. Because anger is often regarded as blameworthy and anti-social, people frequently work hard to suppress its outward manifestations. Unless the source of the anger is dealt with, however, this emotion will find other outlets, like biting humor, hypercriticism, daydreaming, continual but forced jocularity and excessive activity. Eventually, long-suppressed anger may suddenly be released explosively.

The first step to dealing with anger is seeing it as a positive force that can be directed to needed action.

Some anger and blaming are to be expected; however, acting out (or "venting") anger will not relieve it, as is commonly thought, but increase it if the action focuses on the target of the anger.

Physical activity is a good way of working off the adrenaline evoked by anger; humor is also a great tonic. Once the physical side of anger has been calmed down, meditation can lead to a deeper, more lasting cure.

Do not get caught up in the divorcing person's blaming. Instead, encourage him or her to try forgiving the ex-spouse or others in small steps—perhaps some minor habit like snoring or being frequently late. Continuing to blame the ex-spouse for one's troubles has two negative effects: It takes energy away from rebuilding one's life, and it makes one feel like a victim, which prevents one from taking charge of his or her life.

Unfinished Business: Very often, some of the problems that led to a divorce stemmed from unresolved personal problems that predated the marriage—difficulty in expressing feelings; blind, rigid insistence on following rules that made no sense to the spouse; fear of assuming responsibilities; unresolved hostilities, such as those felt by a person who left home with feelings of anger or flight. If these problems are not cleared up, they will spoil any future relationships that the divorced may attempt to form.

As a relative or long-time friend, you may be tied in to this pattern in their lives. This is not to say you must assume responsibility for their divorce. Rather, it is an opportunity to help them grow, and to grow yourself. Approach this not as a counsellor trying to set a client straight but as a partner in your personal relationship with them. Resolving problems with you can carry over into their other relationships.

Children: Young children typically need to be reassured that someone will always take care of them, and that the parent who left still cares about them. If you are a relative from the absent parent's side of the family, maintaining your relationship with them can help them feel a sense of stability. Convincing the parents to work at visitation is important, too.

Children need to understand that they are not responsible for the divorce, and that their parents have not divorced them. Listening to children helps them figure out what is troubling them and helps them to deal with it. Do not attempt to make everything sound "okay"; answer their questions honestly, but avoid giving them more than they can handle.

Older children may feel that their parents have betrayed the values that they inculcated in the children. They need to understand that parents are human, and that their failures do not mean that they are hypocritical. The children may need to be helped through a step-by-step process of forgiveness similar to that suggested for the divorced.

Grandparents can prove particularly helpful in giving the children a sense of their full heritage—for example, by telling the children the important family stories. However, they must be on guard against the trap of "trigenerational enmeshment"—assuming the role of parent over the children or their parent. This will confuse the children and alienate the parent.

Storytelling: Sometimes people want, and ask for, direct advice. More often, however, direct advice makes people defensive or causes them to retrace their circular thoughts. Telling stories about other people allows your friend to consider your information in a more relaxed and objective way.

Storytelling assumes that your friend is capable of recognizing and acting upon good information. Besides telling stories about third parties, you can construct metaphors as a way of getting a point across. For long-term changes in feelings—the slow but essential way of effecting lasting changes in people—repeated general "success" stories can gradually, almost imperceptibly, help them find a new way of looking at their situation.

Our final word of advice is to maintain a proper perspective on your role in divorced people's lives. One common temptation is to react to their pain and confusion by rushing in and taking charge, attempting a "quick fix." This will not work, because their essential task is to take charge of their own lives. The opposite temptation is to conclude that since they must ultimately work out their own problems one cannot really help them and so must leave them to their own devices. This is also likely to fail, because we all need a community of caring people, especially when we are floundering.

St. Paul describes the process of collaboration in this way: "I planted the seed, Apollos watered it, but God made it grow. This means that neither he who plants nor he who waters is of any special account, only God, who gives the growth" (1 Cor 3:6-7).

There can be no growth unless the seed is planted and watered; our help is indispensable. At the same time, we must not feel that everything depends upon us, becoming overly anxious or guilty at a seeming lack of progress. God works through us, but his is the main power at work. As an old adage has it, "Work as if everything depends upon you, but pray as if everything depends upon God."

Bibliography

We encourage you to continue this process of growth that you have started. Allow yourself to gently close the door on this hurt— the divorce of a loved one. Be gentle with yourself. You are created in the image and likeness of God, which means that you are of great value. Give yourself the time to look at related areas in which you can grow and discover new possibilities in your life and relationships. The following annotated bibliography may help.

Catoir, J. *Catholics and Broken Marriage*. Notre Dame, IN: Ave Maria Press, 1979.

Clear and insightful information on the annulment process, offered in a question and answer format. Its pastoral tone suggests that concerned and dedicated people in the church can extend a hand of friendship and support.

Gardner, R. *The Boys and Girls Book About Divorce*. New York, NY: Science House, Inc., 1970.

Written at the junior high school reading level, this is a book many kids can read by themselves. Ideally, however, they can read it with their parents.

Glasser, W. *Control Theory: A New Explanation of How We Control Our Lives*. (Harper & Row Perennial Library, 1985; originally published as *Take Effective Control of Your Life* in 1984).

This helpful book explains how to deal with problems by controlling our interpretations of and reactions to them.

Greteman, J. and Haverkamp, L. *Divorce and Beyond*. Chicago, IL: ACTA Publications, 1983.

Divorce is like entering a strange country without a road map. This book provides a gentle guide.

Greteman, J. *Coping With Divorce*. Notre Dame, IN: Ave Maria Press, 1981 (out of print).

This book offers hope in place of despair and charts the way to self-renewal, to becoming a more fully human, social and religious person.

Kelsey, Morton T. *Caring: How Can We Love One Another?* Mahwah, NJ: Paulist Press, 1981.

A well-written, incisive and practical guide to enriching human relationships.

Kroeger, O., and J. Thuesen. *Type Talk: The Sixteen Personality Types That Determine How We Live, Love and Work*. New York: Delacorte Press, 1988.

This is an accessible discussion of the Myers-Briggs personality types (based on Jung), which can be helpful in understanding and resolving differences with others.

Lerner, H. *The Dance of Anger*. San Francisco: Harper and Row, 1985.

This book, written from a woman's perspective, is a helpful guide to understanding and reducing anger in close relationships.

Lechman, J. *The Spirituality of Gentleness*. San Francisco: Harper and Row, 1987.

The book allows the seeds of wisdom to enter the mind and proceed to the heart—there to be nurtured by the spirit into the actual fruit called gentleness.

Linn, D. and M. *Healing Life's Hurts*. Mahwah, NJ: Paulist Press, 1978.

This book is full of practical suggestions to help the individual get on with the healing of mind, body, and soul.

Peck, M. *The Road Less Traveled*. New York, NY: Simon and Schuster, 1978.

A highly readable book that is valuable and sometimes brilliant in its insistence that there is no distinction between achieving spiritual growth and achieving mental growth. The comments on love are marked by freshness and originality.

Powell, J. *Happiness Is An Inside Job*. Valencia, CA: Tabor Publishing, 1989.

The author describes 10 practices that are necessary in the quest for happiness.

Powell, J. *Why Am I Afraid to Tell You Who I Am?* Valencia, CA: Tabor Publishing, 1969.

An easy-to-read book on how to communicate with others in deeply personal ways.

Ripple, P. *Growing Strong at Broken Places*. Notre Dame, IN: Ave Maria Press, 1986.

This solid, reflective book leads its readers to the understanding that people can experience growth through their suffering. The book helps the reader seek meaning in the pain-filled moments of life.

_____. *The Pain and the Possibility: Divorce and Separation Among Catholics*. Notre Dame, IN: Ave Maria Press, 1978.

An affirming and healing guide for the divorced and separated, their parents and relatives, neighbors and friends.

_____. *Walking With Loneliness*. Notre Dame, IN: Ave Maria Press, 1982.

Offers a message of hope and healing for all who encounter the mystery of loneliness in their lives.

Rupp, J. *Praying Our Goodbyes*. Notre Dame, IN: Ave Maria Press, 1988.

A book for anyone who has experienced loss and seeks to heal the hurts caused by goodbyes and the anxieties encountered by change.

Schaef, A. *Escape From Intimacy*. San Francisco: Harper and Row, 1989.

A book for those who want to embrace intimacy with themselves and others.

Whitehead, E. and J. *A Sense of Sexuality: Christian Love and Intimacy*. New York: Doubleday, 1989.

The book will help you feel better about yourself, deepen your spiritual values and lead a happier and more truly generative life.

What began as an earnest plea—
be~~cont Bme~~ desperate begging for %o
dialogue in June of '94 became
a divorce action in September of 94